Contents   Vol.6 No.4 Autumn 1998

Published by
Labour Co-ordinating Committee Publishing Ltd

In association with
Lawrence & Wishart

ISSN Number 0968-252X

ISBN 0 85315 887 8

Typeset by Derek Doyle & Associates, Mold, Flintshire
Printed and bound in the UK by Postprint, East Harling, Norwich

---

On all matters relating to content (feedback, ideas for future articles etc.) contact either:

Paul Thompson c/o Department of Business Studies
University of Edinburgh William Robertson Building
50 George Square Edinburgh EH8 9JY
tel 0131 650 3811 fax 0131 668 3053 e-mail PaulThompson@ed.ac.uk

Or

Neal Lawson c/o Lawson Lucas Mendelsohn 21a Noel St London W1V 3PD
tel 0171 437 1122 fax 0171 437 7788 email: neal@llm.co.uk

All correspondence or queries relating to subscriptions, promotions and advertising should go to:

Renewal, Lawrence and Wishart 99a Wallis Road London E9 5LN
tel 0181 533 2506 fax 0181 533 7369 email: Renewal@l-w-bks.demon.co.uk

---

Notes on Contributors

Michael Allen lectures at the Cranfield School of Management.

Alice Brown is Professor of Politics at Edinburgh University.

Sue Goss is Director of Public Services Development at the Office of Public Management.

John Grieve Smith is a Fellow of Robinson College, University of Cambrudge.

Gerry Hassan is Director of the Centre for Scottish Public Policy.

Stephanie Hoopes is a lecturer in International Relations and Politics at the University of Sussex. She has recently published *Oil Privatisation, Public Choice and International Forces*, Macmillan, 1997.

Iain MacWhirter is a political correspondent for the Scotsman and presenter of BBC Scotland's Scottish Lobby.

Jim McCormick is Research Director of the Scottish Council Foundation.

Tom Nairn is author of *The Break of Britain* (1981, 2nd ed.), *The Enchanted Glass* (1988), and *Faces of Nationalism* (1997).

Lindsay Paterson is Professor of Educational Policy at Moray House Institute of Education and editor of *Scottish Affairs*.

Barry Quirk is the Chief Executive of the London Borough of Lewisham. (He writes in his personal capacity.)

Mary Southcott has just co-written *Making Votes Count* (Profile Books, 1998) with Martin Linton MP. She researches, writes and speaks about politics, briefing politicians and the media as the Labour Campaign for Electoral Reform's parliamentary and political officer.

Ted Tapper is a reader in Politics at the University of Sussex. His latest book, *Fee-Paying Schools and Educational Change in Britian: Between the State and the Market Place*, was published by Westview Press, 1997.

Not the end of ideology

Paul Thompson

The problems that confront us at home and in the world are resistant to the old terms of ideological debate between 'left' and 'right', and 'ideology' by now, and with good reason, is an irretrievably fallen word.

Anthony Giddens in his new book? Tony Blair at the Third Way summit in Washington? Actually no – Daniel Bell in his seminal *The End of Ideology: On the Exhaustion of Political Ideas in the Fifties*. Seminal but wrong, at least if we have any respect for facts. His 'rough consensus' about Western politics – belief in welfare state, mixed economy, political pluralism – did not last more than a few years after the book was first published in 1960.

When Bell wrote that the old ideologies were exhausted, and had lost their truth and power to persuade, he was, as he admits, talking mainly about the left and Marxism in particular, whose 'terrible simplicities' were incapable of other than formulaic responses to the new realities. Wrong again. For a decade Marxism revitalised and renewed itself before it fell prey to theoretical flaws and fragmentation, combined with the unfortunate fact that, despite increased industrial militancy, the working class wasn't very interested in global proletarian revolution.

The real challenge to the post-war consensus came from the new right whose neo-liberal ideology provided the framework for the dominance of the Thatcher-Reagan axis. While applied deftly to existing circumstances, many of the animating ideas were borrowed unambiguously from the 'old terms of ideological debate'.

Paradoxically, it is primarily this course of events which gives contemporary 'end of ideology' discourses their force and character. These 'old' ideologies have been tried (again) and failed. The old left is marginal and fossilised and the new right dangerous and destructive. Moving beyond their 'terrible simplicities' probably chimes in with the mood of many electorates, tired of political posturing and failed experiments.

Contemporary 'end of ideology' perspectives also lay claim to new, 'new realities' which appear to be beyond left and right – the challenges of globalisation and an information economy. But all may not be what it seems. Ideology traditionally had two meanings: a coherent and systematic set of ideas, and a means to define and organise a set of interests. With those in place, it could act as a lever for action, necessarily mediating between values and policies. In these senses the Third Way is classically ideological. The Gidden's book (1998) and the Blair pamphlet (1998) for the Fabians are far more coherent and thoughtful analyses than their critics credit. Moreover the identification of ideas and values is clearly aimed at providing a basis to act on the real world, not just at differentiating philosophies. The Third Way is not ideological in the Marxist sense that assumes tight relationships between interests and agencies, but the ideas and practices are seen as underpinning new alliances to sustain a durable left-of-centre project.

However, on the road to the Third Way there are no such enemies against whom you need to adopt an ideology by which to define yourself. Classes, parties and interests have again been cast into the post-ideological dustbin. Everything can be reconciled – rights and responsibilities, promotion of enterprise and the attack on poverty; while the only enemies are values: cynicism, fatalism and prejudice (Blair 1998). The New Labour project appears to want it both ways, to be an 'ideology for an age which has rejected ideologies' (Tony Wright, *Prospect*, October 1998).

New Labour governance: experts, fixers and wonks?

Tony Wright goes on to argue that a danger of trying to avoid ideology is that 'politics soon becomes merely about place and position'. This, of course, is the insult thrown most often against New Labour inside and outside Parliament. It surfaced most strongly in 'cronygate'. During that hiatus, Polly Toynbee referred to the flotilla of young men for whom policies are simply the tools of power: 'There is no right or wrong, no ideology, not even "what works" in the real world. For them all that works is the selling of messages ...' (*The Guardian*, 8 July 1998). Ignore for a moment that Polly Toynbee helped launched the SDP – the classic vehicle for stodgy, non-ideological consensus politics and ambitious bandwagon jumpers of all ages and persuasions – she has a point.

The impression sometimes given during these events was that Labour's accession to office meant merely a different seventeen people 'who really count', a changing of the guard in and to the political class. But we shouldn't exaggerate the dangers of lobbying, which, if properly regulated, is a legitimate, if occasionally unedifying, part of any democratic system. Nor should we construct explanations of everyone's behaviour and motives as being based solely on Derek Draper's big mouth and wide-boy political philosophy.

The thing that struck home to me during these events was not so much the impression that New Labour meant business as usual, but the absence of any critique of business. 'Old Labour' dogmatically could never find anything good to say about markets and businesses, but that does not mean that modernisers have to stand that 'wisdom' on its head. After all, is there nothing that needs radical modernisation in the business world? As Michael Allen points out, it is British employers, rather than unions, who are often now 'behind the times' in refusing to enter into modern mutual gains industrial relations arrangements. It seems to me that this wilful blindness does have something to do with ideology. For example there is the widely-quoted example of the lobby company that defines ideology as part of the 'passing world' (along with conviction, ownership etc), to be replaced by pragmatism and values. I wonder how far these arguments square with the actual behaviour of the clients of such lobbyists. For instance, what price the oft-repeated argument that ownership doesn't matter when Murdoch has to buy Manchester United in order to further rig the global communications market?

Of course the Government is not the same as its friendly lobbyists. But the wider issues are not just about lobbyists, but of the nature of the contemporary political class. As a number of commentators, such as Hugo Young and Iain MacWhirter, have noted, there is an increasing merging of the worlds of politics, public relations, lobbying and the media. The core expertise is often that of presentation, with conviction politics largely taking a back seat to the politics of personality. All politics, not just that practised from Millbank, fashions a culture of fix and spin, but New Labour has made this into something of an art form. While no guarantee of purity or truth, ideology is one of the protective layers against the corruption and reproduction of power.

Even the most ardent spinner would not claim his or her art to be the essence of good governance. New Labour also tends to pride itself on being pragmatic. As Charlie Leadbeater noted in *New Times*, 'I think the dominant ethos of the Government is probably one of managerial competence'. Now nobody in their right mind wants incompetence, and further, pragmatism about means is surely sensible. But one problem is that efficiency and expertise have often appeared to be associated only with business and businesspeople. This can be seen in the large number of such figures drafted into government. The concept of expertise detached from ideology is problematic. How committed to and guided by core social democratic values are those captains of industry and commerce? It is also part of a wider tendency to bypass the normal political process of parliament and party; magnified by a large majority and the ease by which conventional checks and balances can be avoided and evaded.

Labour should promote a distinctive, radical mode of governance and in many senses it does. At its best, the Government has promoted an innovative values-based approach, willing to experiment and careful to make the process inclusive. This can be seen in the collaboration with the Liberal Democrats, in Northern Ireland, in the moves towards devolution and decentralisation of power, and in the listening style personified by the Prime Minister. The simple truth and complex reality is that there are many faces of Labour governance – it is in Charlie Leadbeater's words 'many headed'. When it doesn't act in these ways, its actions must be made transparent and accountable through the normal checks and balances of political life. As Sue Goss argues, trust is not enough; we need some new as well as old rules of engagement between state, business and civil society.

A heightening of ideological awareness will be necessary to meet the range of substantial challenges facing Labour in the forthcoming period, two of which are discussed in this issue: electoral reform and the new Scottish Parliament.

New challenges

At the time of writing, the content of the Jenkins proposals on electoral reform are not known, though a variant of AV-plus, combining direct constituency voting with an indirect top-up from party lists, appears to be the front runner. I have to confess that I am not as sanguine about the redemptive qualities of PR as I used to be – the idea that it *necessarily* gets rid of adversarial politics, fosters co-operation and allows us to hear a greater diversity of voices is belied by too many concrete experiences. Spending some time in New Zealand last year cured me of any illusions in these respects. Their PR arrangements have had almost none of the intended benefits and a lot of unwanted outcomes, notably as New Zealand First cynically broke its promises and hitched its star to the neo-liberal National Party.

There are still powerful arguments in favour of electoral reform. It is in principle wrong that, for example, the Tories have no representation in Scotland and Wales. As Mary Southcott argues (in this issue), when people's votes don't count it fundamentally damages the legitimacy of democratic politics. It is not beyond the whit of current or future policy makers to devise arrangements that retain a prominent direct link to local constituencies, while allowing for a fairer relationship between voters' wishes and electoral outcomes.

But all the arguments about content and timing of any referendum are in one sense missing the point. Labour has already changed the political landscape by introducing a variety of forms of PR for Europe, Scotland, Northern Ireland, and potentially for local government. *Any* form of PR will make that landscape more ideologically-based than it is at present. Such systems encourage political fragmentation and therefore sharpen the terms of competition. Splits in the two grand coalitions are highly likely: Tories to the right, Labour to the left. Parties are, therefore, under pressure to re-define their core message and constituencies of support. The diminution of the need to focus primarily on swing voters in marginal seats should allow them the space to do so.

The importance of the terms of competition can be seen in contemporary Scottish politics. There are simple, conventional reasons why the SNP vote has surged since the devolution referendum. Buoyed by its dual success Labour took its eye off the ball and became complacent. But something more complex is also going on. However misleadingly, the SNP has positioned itself to the left of Labour, seeking to detach sections of the latter's more traditional 'old Labour' support. Electorally this makes a lot of sense, particularly under PR, with second preference votes up for grabs.

It is possible to exaggerate the differences between the Scottish and English electorates, particularly if the comparison is with Labour's urban, northern heartlands. But, as our articles in this issue demonstrate, there is evidence of distinctiveness, in particular among a salariat that is more collectivist and liberal, and a civil society that is broadly more social democratic. While Labour's modernising agenda does resonate with the concerns of many voters, its ideological message has been cutting partly against the grain. This is amplified by the specifically national dimension. Bluntly, the Party is perceived to be not Scottish enough, and this is about ideology, not policy. On the latter, a sustained bout of Nat-bashing and increased firepower from Helen Liddell and co. appears to have had the desired effect. Changing the underlying message may not be as easy as changing the label to *Scottish* New Labour.

The Party needs to change the substance of the ideological and policy framework to address specifically Scottish issues in a distinctive way. More importantly it needs to be given space by the Party as a whole, to do so. This is more a question of practical politics than the nuances of political philosophy. A devolved parliament requires a changed strategy and the electorate will punish Labour if it does not produce one. Freed from the dual tyranny of UK and Tory domination, the Scottish electorate is experimenting with more complex expressions of its interests and desires. It is pointless to wish the genie back into the bottle. As all our contributors show in this issue, the political landscape has not just been changed in Scotland, but in the rest of the UK too. There is a challenge for Labour to develop new identities for the British state and the English nation.

The Labour co-ordinating committee: end of an era?

It may not be the end of ideology, but it could soon be the end for the Labour Co-ordinating Committee (LCC). The spawning of this journal is not the least of its achievements in a fifteen-year period during which it has been at the heart of the modernisation process. There are three essential pre-conditions for the existence and effectiveness of a pressure group: a distinctive and independent political project, the human and financial resources to carry it out, and a context sufficiently favourable to make such activities worthwhile.

Given the current configuration of political forces, it might seem odd that its Executive Committee is to recommend winding up the organisation. But it is precisely that configuration that is the problem. There are so many of the troops inside the machine – as MPs, advisors, organisers, lobbyists – that the willingness, ability and energy to articulate distinctive perspectives and organise for them has become progressively disabled.

There is no reason why any organisation should last for ever and there may well be a view that the LCC's job is done. It is, therefore, unfortunate, that its imminent demise coincides with the re-emergence of the hard left, at least if the results of the NEC elections are anything to go by. While the willingness to pick and mix from the slates was neither surprising or unwelcome, the results were in some ways depressing. Many members were willing to vote for candidates such as Willsman and Davies whose politics brought the Party to the brink of (self) destruction in the 1980s. That those who had opposed every one-member, one-vote reform were able to pose as defenders of party democracy without producing hysterical laughter or undisguised contempt indicates a substantial collective memory loss.

But what was really depressing was the predictability of the outcome. For all the hard left smears of 'Kinnockites' etc, in the heady days when the LCC used to organise the soft left slate, it was rightly perceived as having something independent to say. It should not be forgotten that the LCC and its allies defeated the hard left politically as well as organisationally. Since 1983 the latter has spent its time defending yesterday's positions rather than developing feasible and well-thought out alternatives to the new orthodoxies. In the past few years the LCC's own version of the end of ideology has removed much of that advantage. At the same time its unwillingness to respond to legitimate concerns about centralising tendencies, with the attendant manipulation and squeezing of dissent, has opened up the franchise for listening to and advancing the views of the 'grassroots'.

The chickens have thus now come home to roost for the soft left. The view that the machine can act without the wider Party through direct communication with members and voters is seductive, but shallow. And, as Andy McSmith (*The Observer*, 23 August) notes, even Tony Blair needs a political base in the Party. Whether or how the LCC will be replaced organisationally is anyone's guess, though it is clear that NEC elections cannot be won by Millbank fronts. Organisations are politics in action. There is a distinctive modernising left perspective – economically egalitarian and interventionist, socially libertarian and politically pluralist – but unless this is recovered and developed, results like the 1998 NEC will continue.

An end to neo-liberalism?

So if there is no end to ideology in general, is there an end to neo-liberalism in particular? After all, with the victory of the German Social Democrats, we have left-of-centre governments in most of the major European countries.

Unfortunately it is not as simple as this: neo-liberalism as ideology is well embedded in practices and institutions. While the new generation of social democratic leaders are genuinely searching for a role, albeit reduced, for active government, there are few signs of a desire to reverse the de-regulationist tide. In part this is pragmatic. Governments must live within the existing rules of the international game where one false move could bring a recession nearer. At the same time those rules are clearly inadequate to cope with current financial and economic crises. While concern is growing, the ideological hold of past orthodoxies remains strong. In their otherwise admirable speeches to Party conference, Gordon Brown and Tony Blair continued to talk of the operation of global markets as either benign or inexorable. However, as Will Hutton argues, 'The financial markets have achieved their awesome power not because it is inevitable that they should have such power; they have been accorded it because governments have been told and become convinced that the state should not have it' (*The Observer*, 13 October). The social democratic governments of Europe have an unprecedented opportunity to change the terms of debate and policy. Third Way debates are an important contribution to this process. But in their existing form and with their weaknesses in terms of political economy, the renewal of social democracy will need additional sources and inspiration.

References

Tony Blair (1998) *The Third Way: New Politics for the New Century*, Fabian Society.
Anthony Giddens (1998) *The Third Way*, Cambridge, Polity Press.

Scotland: an unwon cause?

Gerry Hassan

The first Scottish Parliament election campaign has already begun: this is clear from the twin Labour appointments of Helen Liddell and Gus MacDonald at the Scottish Office aimed at giving more sense of direction and greater weight when laying into the Nats. The process of devolution is already changing Scotland with Labour's one party local fiefdoms being brought under a new degree of scrutiny, while Scottish Labour's electoral hegemony is facing its first serious challenge in forty years from a confident and resurgent SNP.

How Scotland has changed

The election of a Labour government in May 1997 witnessed the most emphatic ever Scottish result in a general election with the forces of constitutional change returned in every one of the 72 Scottish constituencies, with the Tories reduced to no parliamentary representation. Five months later, a landslide 'Yes, Yes' vote in the referendum seemed to produce a new dawn in Scottish politics: a nation where the three parties in favour of constitutional change – Labour, the Lib Dems and the SNP – could maturely sit down, talk and work together. This vote produced a brief moment where Scottish and British Labour seemed in harmony, Donald Dewar was held in universal regard across the political spectrum, and Tony Blair was seen in Scotland as an unquestioned asset.

This seems like a long time ago. What has gone wrong for Scottish Labour? A number of short-term factors have influenced the political climate. There has been the constant drip of old Labour sleaze: Sarwar, Tommy Graham, Glasgow, North Lanarkshire, etc. West of Scotland Labour has faced an unprecedented degree of scrutiny because the Tories have gone and devolution is coming, and it has been exacerbated by Labour's failure to act conclusively in many of these cases: talking tough and then dithering for periods of up to eighteen months. This was shown at its worst in the party's failure to remove Pat Lally from the largely ceremonial role of Lord Provost of Glasgow City Council.

Also, there have been problems with the New Labour agenda. Put at its most basic, New Labour is seen by many Scots both as an English phenomenon with no relevance to Scotland and also as the direct descendant of Thatcherism. However, while both of these factors have contributed to Scottish Labour's fall from grace, more profound factors are at work which will be more difficult for the party to turn around in the run-up to the first Scottish Parliament elections.

First, the idea of 'Scottishing' politics north of the border, while having short-comings as an analysis, does address that the forthcoming Parliament elections are first and foremost elections where the competing parties will have to position themselves as Scottish parties. Second, the defeat of the Tories and election of a Labour government has changed the dynamics of Scottish politics. When the Tories were in power, Scottish Labour was a natural vehicle for nationalist protest and acted as a buffer against the SNP. With the demise of the Tories Labour can no longer fulfil this role; thus the SNP can now better position themselves as the party best served to represent Scotland's interests. Third, a Scottish nationalist agenda which cut across all Scotland's political parties defined Scottish politics in the 1980s. Scottish Labour and the Scottish Lib Dems saw themselves as part of this, signing *A Claim of Right* and launching the Scottish Constitutional Convention. But such a kind of politics proves more difficult to translate to the politics of British government. Fourth, the decline of the Tories and Lib Dems has allowed the SNP to position itself as the repository of anti-Labour voters and the main beneficiary of a re-alignment of Scottish politics from an asymmetrical system of Labour dominance to a competitive two party contest where Labour's long held dominance is now being seriously challenged.

The first Scottish Parliament elections

The Scottish Parliamentary elections will be seen as primarily a Labour-SNP contest. The outcome of this will be determined not by the rival policy prospectuses, but by a combination of positioning, media and marketing strategies. Considering that Labour and the SNP share much common ground on centre-left post-Thatcherite agendas, the parties will engage in the kind of Presidential personality contests that characterise much of what passes for political debate in Western societies – Dewar vs. Salmond – while flinging insult upon insult at each other about tax and spending plans and the merits of devolution vs. independence. A key element in deciding the victor will be which party can best present itself as standing up for Scotland's interests: a June poll by MORI found 43 per cent saw Scottish Labour as standing up for Scotland compared to 77 per cent for the SNP (*The Scotsman*, 5 June 1998).

Predictably, and to disastrous effect, Scottish Labour strategy has been non-existent since the general election. The party seems to have no sense of direction or vision, lacking any consistent idea of how to deal with the SNP, while seeming to many to be under the control of a Blair leadership which has little feel or understanding for the complexities of Scottish politics. And I am sure that, from London, Blair is equally mystified about what has gone wrong in Scotland and has a sense of anger about the mutual incomprehension both sides of the border. Even in opposition this was touched upon by Blair when, in 1996, he called the Scottish media 'unreconstructed wankers'.

How does Labour begin to dig itself out this hole? Firstly, any approach has to be Scottish based and designed. Second, Blair's 'Middle Scotland', while right in many ways, is politically doomed because it comes from Blair and is seen as dictated by 'Middle England' priorities, thus failing on both counts of the first point. Third, any strategy for dealing with the SNP has to recognise that for the last thirty years consistent majorities of Scots have seen the SNP as good for Scotland, so consequently the 'bashing the Nats' approach is counterproductive and should be abandoned by Labour. Finally, Labour needs to put in place a Scottish 'Operation Victory' which includes not just organisational efficiency, but political priorities. The crucial swing group of voters in May 1999 are the 'Salmond-Labour' voters – people who have previously voted Labour or still will at a Westminster level, but are considering voting SNP for Holyrood. This group, like 'Reagan Democrats' or 'Basildon Man' could decide the outcome of the election and become symbolic of the new political age Scotland is entering, and its emerging political coalitions.

The potential of the Parliament

Many supporters of a Scottish Parliament have long hoped that its arrival would see the dawning of a new politics where civil society and the Parliament worked together in harmony. This view misjudges the characteristics of Scottish civil society which is driven by a consensual conformity and distorted by Labour's hold over much of Scots public life (Hassan 1998). The Parliament and civil society may choose to emphasise their similarities or differences with each other: Parliament could challenge civil society as paternalist and parochial, while civil society could claim that *it* rather than the Parliament best represents popular sovereignty.

Lindsay Paterson, in his contribution to this issue, argues that a parliament with a Labour influenced majority would see the SNP present the problem as Scotland not being sufficiently independent of England. It would attempt to utilise the potential of civil society as the guardian of a Scots autonomy denied by Labour's subservience to London. An SNP influenced majority, including the defenders of Scots distinctiveness, would challenge Labour dominated civil society, perhaps acting as a Scots centre-left equivalent of Thatcherism, and criticising a Labour dominated civil society as the source of most of Scotland's problems. This strategy has been made all the more plausible by the Labour sleaze stories in the past year.

According to SNP thinking, there are two possible scenarios post-devolution which could lead to independence. In the first, the success of devolution leads to increased Scots self-confidence and eventually to Scottish independence. In the second, devolution is shaped more by external factors and conflict than internal factors and a Scottish agenda, leading to devolution failing. As Jim McCormick observes, the demand for independence is driven more by a sense of grievance than satisfaction. If this is true, devolution implies a watershed for the SNP, of either remaining a party stuck to old fashioned ideas of statehood and constantly running the risk of being accused as wreckers, or of developing into a nationalist party which accepts that the Scots nation does not need the trappings of statehood. Salmond has hinted at the latter, but it is still a long journey for the SNP, which would need him to stand up to his fundamentalist wing in a way for which, so far, he has shown no appetite.

A much neglected influence on Scotland is the role of Britain and British identities and nationalisms. Tom Nairn is dismissive of the degree of change and innovation at the heart of 'New Britain' and suspicious of the radicalism in Labour's constitutional programme as long as it does not address the English Question. What cannot be disputed here is that the conclusion of the different agencies and actors at a British level and within New Labour has implications for Scotland's constitutional future.

Scottish politics, culture and society are about to embark on a new era which requires new thinking and outlooks. Strange then that many at the heart of this debate, in the Labour Party, SNP, trade unions, or the voluntary sector, see this great project as one which demands no new thinking or practice. This view is held because these groups see the Parliament as an open licence for maintaining the existing Scottish social democratic settlement which has survived Thatcherism. This is the road of early and bitter disillusionment, where the Scots professional classes and sections of civil society maintain their block on the kind of radical change which opens up Scotland and aids innovation and diversity.

This requires new political paradigms which are different from those which flourished during Scotland's eighteen years of Tory rule. Then, a broad based Scots nationalism flourished across large parts of Scottish life; today, new narratives are required which acknowledge the Scottish and British identities of most Scots. This needs new kinds of unionisms and nationalisms which are more fluid and less certain than the ones we are used to dealing with. Scottish unionism is still seen as synonymous with Thatcherism, but if the no surrender mentality of the Ulster Unionists can engage in creative revisionism, then surely there is hope for the Scots.

The interventions of Andrew Neil (1998) and Bill Jamieson (1998) seem to represent nothing here but the death knell of an old, intemperate unionism which has little understanding of contemporary Scotland. This is important because it has consequences beyond the Scottish Tories, for all Scotland's parties. Scottish Labour has throughout its history been influenced by different kinds of unionism and national-ism, and the party's success will be in part measured by how it manages to find a new modus operandi between the two. A new kind of unionism for Scotland in the new 'Union-state' is a prerequisite to making home rule work (Mitchell 1998).

The constitutional options of devolution and independence are not, of course, really as clear cut as their Labour and SNP supporters would like to pretend they are. The debate between George Kerevan and Andrew Marr (1998) in *Prospect* magazine showed that an increasingly assertive and successful home rule parliament would soon begin to blur the boundaries between what in today's world are traditional and slightly obsolescent concepts of devolution and independence. It is, of course, as Alice Brown observes, up to the Scottish people whether the current Scotland Bill will turn out to represent 'the settled will of the Scottish people', but what is certain is that Scotland is moving towards an imagined independence of the mind, what Tom Nairn calls a 'de facto independence'. If this is to be the eventual new terrain of Scottish politics, then Scottish Labour must start moving fast, developing fresh thinking and ideas if it is not to be as out-manoeuvred in the future as it has in the past year by the SNP.

This issue of *Renewal* builds on a recent conference by the Centre for Scottish Public Policy, 'The New Scotland', sponsored by the *Herald*, *New Statesman* and Fabian Society. The event brought together Donald Dewar, Jim Wallace and Alex Salmond, with a variety of politicians, academics and commentators. From these debates and contributions, it is imperative that Scottish politics gets down to serious and detailed policy debates and choices. This requires taking on board the unwilling-ness of Scottish politicians so far to engage in this debate, and that the fierce compe-tition between Labour and SNP for votes makes it even less likely.

Policy and research work by Scotland's intellectual communities will not, by their nature, always have an easy relationship with party politicians, and in a small coun-try like Scotland we will have to manage and celebrate a culture of debate and argu-ment more effectively than we sometimes have. However, difficult questions have to be asked about Scotland's future which party politicians would sometimes want to avoid, and the Scottish debate, if it is to mean anything, has to address how the Parliament can make a measurable difference to the quality of life. It is going to be a bumpy and nervous year ahead, full of tension and on-message politics, but we have to bring policy options into the debate and a sense of vision and hope about the prospects ahead.

References

Hassan, G. (1998), *The New Scotland*, London, Fabian Society.

Jamieson, B. (1998), *The Bogus State of Brigadoon*, London, Centre for Policy Studies.

Kerevan, G. and Marr, A. (1998), 'Is Home Rule Enough?', *Prospect*, August/ September 1998, pp 18-21.

Mitchell, J. (1998), 'Contemporary Unionism', in MacDonald, C.M.M,. (ed.), *Unionist Scotland 1800-1997*, Glasgow, John Donald.

Neil, A. (1998), 'Scotland the Self-Deluded', *Spectator*, 15 August 1998, pp 11-12.

The changing shape of Scottish politics and Scottish identities

Alice Brown

In 1999, some 300 years since the Treaty of Union, a new parliament will be estab-lished in Scotland, or as the first clause of the 1997 Scotland Bill put it, 'There shall be a Scottish Parliament'. Not only will this be a crucial event in Scottish history but it will herald another significant phase in the development of Scottish politics. Until relatively recently political commentators have tended to assume that politics in Scotland was just a smaller version of British politics, with perhaps the existence of the SNP as a minor complication. This is an assumption that has been challenged in the past (Brown *et al* 1998a), and it is certainly one that will be totally unsustainable in the future. With the setting up of a Scottish Parliament, people will have the oppor-tunity to vote separately for the Westminster and Scottish Parliaments. The elections for the Parliament in Scotland will operate under the Additional Member System – a more proportional system. Therefore, for the first time ever, the electorate will be able to split their votes between two political parties. Such changes are likely to impact on the party system in Scotland and will mean that the distinctive nature of Scottish politics is also likely to increase.

Events have moved quickly since the Labour election victory of May 1997 when the Conservative Party lost all of its parliamentary seats in Scotland. The White Paper on devolution was published by the government in July 1997. The results of the refer-endum which followed in September were, according to the Secretary of State, Donald Dewar, beyond his wildest dreams. Over 74 per cent of those who voted in the referendum agreed that a Scottish Parliament should be established and, perhaps more surprisingly, more than 64 per cent also agreed that the Parliament should have tax varying powers. In accordance with the government's planned timetable, the Scotland Bill was published in December 1997 before being presented to the House of Commons in January 1998. The first elections are to be held in May 1999 with the first sitting of the Parliament in July of the same year.

The existence of a Scottish Parliament will change substantially the political context in which party politics are played out, as well as providing a new political agenda within which Scottish politics takes place. As a result of these political developments, Scottish politics will never be the same again. The focus of this article is the changing shape of Scottish politics and Scottish identities. It discusses the role of civil society in constitutional developments before drawing on survey data from the 1997 Scottish Election Survey and the Scottish Referendum Survey in order to provide some understanding of why political events took the form they did and what they might lead to in the future.

The role of civil society

Scottish civil society has played a significant role in developing plans for constitutional change and in shaping Scottish identity. As Lindsay Paterson (1994) has discussed, this role is not confined to modern politics. Since the Union of 1707, the governance of Scotland evolved and changed through a process of 'negotiated compromise' in which civic institutions helped maintain the country's separate identity and autonomy. After the election of the first Thatcher government in 1979, this system came under increasing pressure and the power of civil society was challenged. Such a challenge was interpreted as an attack on Scotland (McCrone 1992) and on Scottish identity and autonomy.

One particular group, the Campaign for a Scottish Parliament (CSP) was instrumental in pressing for home rule and in establishing the Scottish Constitutional Convention in 1989. Other groups emerged after plans for home rule were thwarted with the re-election of the Conservative government in 1992, including Scotland United, Democracy for Scotland, Common Cause and the Coalition for Scottish Democracy; and a Scottish Civic Assembly was set up in 1994. The Constitutional Convention sought to build a consensus around plans for home rule and brought together Labour and the Liberal Democrats in Scotland together with representatives of numerous bodies in civil society, including local government, trade unions, churches, the voluntary sector, women's organisations and others. Many of the proposals contained in the Convention's final report, *Scotland's Parliament, Scotland's Right* (SCC, 1995), were later incorporated into the new government's White Paper on Devolution. The Parliament would have 129 members elected by proportional representation (AMS); the power to legislate in a whole range of domestic policies including education and training, economic development, health, housing, law and home affairs, and local government; and the ability to vary taxation.

Civil society has, therefore, grown accustomed to playing a part in politics and the evolving process of change. Different groups are considering how they can continue to influence the debate. Other organisations who have been less involved in the past are recognising that, with the creation of a parliament in Scotland, the rules of the game will alter. They too are considering how they will be affected and can respond to the changing political environment. Similarly, professional lobby firms were not slow in anticipating the opportunities offered by a new legislature.

One vehicle that has been used to sustain the dialogue with civil society is the all-party Consultative Steering Group set up by the Secretary of State for Scotland in 1998. As well as representatives from the four main political parties, the group includes people nominated by the Convention and COSLA (Convention of Scottish Local Authorities) and others representing different interests from the trade union movement, the business sector, consumers and equal opportunities. The group is consulting more widely through inviting written submissions, and holding Open Forums in different parts of Scotland, with specific events targeted at young people in the community. The group has been asked to gather evidence and put forward recommendations for standing orders and procedures for the new parliament based on principles of power-sharing, accountability, accessibility, openness and responsiveness and the operation of equal opportunities. It will be a matter for the first elected members of the Parliament to make the final decisions on parliamentary arrangements, but the hope and expectations of campaigners are that standing orders and procedures will differ markedly from the Westminster model, and that the balance of power between the parties and the people and the Scottish Parliament will be different.

What do the people say?

The 1997 Scottish Election Survey and the Referendum Survey provide evidence of the political behaviour and attitudes of the electorate in Scotland, their political values, their policy preferences, and the extent to which views on a Scottish Parliament influenced voting behaviour and the referendum result. Previous surveys and opinion polls tended to ask respondents to rank constitutional change along with other policies such as employment, housing and education. Not surprisingly, it did not rank highly in a list of social policies. The 1997 studies took a different approach by separating the questions; and focusing on what people thought constitutional change would deliver.

Political behaviour and attitudes

The key questions examined were: does the social structure of Scotland explain voting behaviour; does social structure affect voting in Scotland in the same ways in which it affects voting south of the border; to what extent do social identities take precedence over social location as explanations of voting behaviour; and in what ways do identities in Scotland overlap to reinforce or cross-cut each other? Comparing voting patterns in 1997 in Scotland with those at the 1992 election and with patterns in the rest of Britain, there is little evidence to suggest that voters in Scotland were any more volatile than those elsewhere in Britain. In terms of either voting for the same party at both elections or abstaining, 67 per cent of those in Scotland and 65 per cent of those in the rest of Britain behaved in the same way at both elections. A majority of people who claimed an identification with a party also voted for that party. Differences in the reasons given for voting in Scotland as compared with the rest of Britain are relatively small, as are changes in the patterns of party support between 1992 and 1997. The Scots were no more likely to be vote switchers, despite having a greater number of parties from which to choose, although tactical voting was more likely to favour the Liberal Democrats in the rest of Britain.

Examining the impact of social structure, it is clear that voting behaviour cannot be explained solely in terms of class location. For example, amongst the salariat in England and Wales, equal proportions voted for Labour and the Conservatives, whilst in Scotland a higher proportion of the salariat voted Labour than Conservative. SNP support among the different classes is not strongly differentiated. Although their support is lowest among the petty bourgeoisie and highest among the working class, the differences are small. Further examination of the influence of housing tenure, educational level, age and gender show that the relationship between social location measures and voting behaviour is weak.

There has been renewed interest in social identities as an explanation of voting behaviour in Scotland in recent years. In Scotland, levels of working-class identity have tended to be higher than elsewhere in Britain (Brand, *et al* 1994) even after the occupational breakdown is taken into account. Religion has also been an important influence on voting in Scotland in the past. More recently, national identity has grown alongside religious and class identities as an explanation for the Scottish vote. The evidence from the surveys suggests that identities are both cross-cutting and reinforcing. A relationship between class identity and voting behaviour is clear, with the Conservatives doing better amongst those who think of themselves as middle-class and Labour amongst those who think of themselves as working-class. The Liberal Democrats in Scotland are more likely to gain support from those who consider themselves to be middle-class, while the SNP is more likely to benefit from those who consider themselves to be working-class. In terms of the relationship between vote and religion, the historical link between Labour and Catholic voters in Scotland remains, with Labour having two-thirds of the Catholic vote. In Scotland, unlike England, there is a clear relationship between national identity and vote, perhaps due to the fact that the issue has been politicised in Scotland. Using the scale 'Scottish not British', 'More Scottish than British', 'Equally Scottish and British', 'More British than Scottish', 'British not Scottish', the Conservatives do not do well among those with a predominantly Scottish identity. Not surprisingly, the SNP poll highest among those with an exclusive Scottish identity. Labour do well amongst all groups, but their support is lower among the minority of the Scottish electorate who felt more British than Scottish.

To conclude, relatively weak influence of social structure on voting behaviour was found, with few differences in this respect between Scotland and the rest of Britain. A partial explanation for the distinctiveness of the election results in Scotland can be found in the feelings of identity held by the Scottish electorate. But this is not the whole story.

Political values

Moving on to look at political values in Scotland, evidence from the data reinforces findings of previous research showing that Scotland is different in terms of value scales, being more socialist, more liberal and less British nationalist than the rest of Britain. Within Scotland itself, the figures would suggest that there is relatively little regional variation, with the exception that the socialist scale is more significant in the West Central region of Scotland. While Conservative voters in Scotland and England are not different in their values, Labour voters in Scotland are significantly more left-wing than their counterparts south of the border and also significantly less national-istic in terms of their attitudes towards the British state. Part of the success of the SNP, and to some extent the Labour Party in Scotland, can be explained by the polit-ical discourse of linking Scottish nationalism with left-wing attitudes. This helps rein-force the perception that to be right wing is to be anti-Scottish, a perception that works to the disadvantage of the Conservative Party in Scotland. Testing this latter proposition by examining people's level of trust in the parties to work in Scotland's interests, we can see that over 90 per cent of respondents who were non-Conservative identifiers expected that the Conservative Party would work in Scotland's interest 'only some of the time' or 'almost never'. This helps explain the poor showing of the Conservatives in the 1997 election. Not only are they viewed negatively because of their policy positions and their political values, they are viewed negatively because they are perceived as anti-Scottish.

Policy preferences

It is a commonly held view that policy preferences in Scotland differ significantly from those in the rest of Britain. The Scottish Election Survey asked respondents about their preferences in the areas of health policy, education, law and order, the environment, distribution of income and wealth, poverty, taxation, trade union and labour market laws, nationalisation, defence and overseas aid. The general first impression from the findings is one of uniformity across the nations of Britain; and also that the whole of Britain remains broadly social democratic. However, there are some areas where the intensity of feeling in Scotland differs, most clearly in relation to the debate over the future of the welfare state. Scots are more likely than people in England to favour government action to end poverty or to redis-tribute wealth. They are also more likely to favour a statutory minimum wage. The Scots are more supportive of state ownership of industry and more in favour of Britain's signing up to the European Union's Social Chapter. Most notably the

Scots are more likely to oppose selection for secondary schooling, and they are more hostile to the private sector in education. An important feature of these results is that, with the exception of education, the differences are mainly in areas that will not be devolved to the Scottish Parliament, such as taxation and redistribution.

Exploring the explanations for the difference in policy preferences between Scotland and the rest of Britain, there is evidence to suggest that this is because certain aspects of policy have become closely linked to feelings about Scottish national identity and the political reactions to policies pursued by the Conservative governments in office during the 1980s and 1990s.

Views on a Scottish Parliament

Constitutional change was an important aspect of the debate during the general election in Scotland. The Labour Party promised that if it won the election, it would pursue its plans for reform and hold a referendum. As stated above, a majority of Scots voted Yes/Yes in the referendum for a Scottish Parliament with tax varying powers. In the Scottish Referendum Study we sought to explore why people voted the way they did in the referendum and the influence of the issue on the general election results. Explanations based on a rational choice model of voting or social location are not supported by the evidence. The findings would suggest that a model of welfare rationality best explains the result of the referendum. Most strikingly, contrary to the view that higher taxes will act as a disincentive to voters, the majority of people in Scotland voted Yes/Yes in the referendum despite expecting higher taxes. They did so on the basis that they thought the Parliament would have a positive effect on the economy, unemployment, education, the NHS, and welfare. So it would seem that people in Scotland voted for a Parliament with tax varying powers because they believed it would bring benefits to Scotland in terms of social welfare.

In this context, the Conservatives' attempt to frighten people away from voting, for Labour in the general election, or for other parties who supported constitutional change, on the grounds of the threat of the 'Tartan Tax' or threat to Britishness was unsuccessful. Indeed the evidence would suggest that the stance of the Conservative Party on the constitutional question contributed to their loss of votes. They lost the argument both with the electorate as a whole, and with people who generally thought of themselves as Conservative supporters. This would suggest that if they are to regain support in Scotland then the Conservative Party will have to find ways of working constructively within the new parliament.

The future

So far we have concentrated on the distinctiveness of Scottish political behaviour and attitudes in the past. Speculation surrounds the extent to which constitutional change will impact on Scottish politics in the future. How will the Labour Party manage policy differences north and south of the border? Will there inevitably be conflict between the Scottish Parliament and Westminster? How will the electorate vote in the first elections for the new parliament? Will devolution be the 'stepping stone' or 'slippery slope' to independence?

We have already discussed the way in which groups and organisations in civil society have played a key and important role in campaigning for home rule and in devising a scheme for the future governance of Scotland. They wish to continue to play such a role and to support plans for power sharing and making the Parliament more open, transparent and democratically accountable to people in Scotland. There is much talk about engendering a 'new politics' and consensus-building around common objectives. Whether such aspirations will be met is the subject of another discussion.

What is clear is that the operation of the new electoral system for the first elections to the Scottish Parliament will affect the hegemony that the Labour Party has traditionally enjoyed in Scottish politics. As the Secretary of State, Donald Dewar, acknowledged: 'The changes to the electoral system are by any standards brave and, indeed, some of my less charitable party colleagues regard the proportional electoral system as a form of charitable giving almost without precedent in Scottish politics' (Dewar, 1998, p.9). Initial calculations, based on the 1997 general election results, indicated that although Labour would be the largest party, it would not have an overall majority. Since that time opinion poll evidence has shown that the electorate are likely to distinguish between elections for Westminster and elections for the Scottish Parliament, a distinction that could operate against Labour in Scotland. While voting intentions for Westminster still have Labour ahead of the SNP, those for the Scottish Parliament now show the SNP ahead of Labour (for example, in June, the SNP was ahead of Labour for the Scottish Parliament by 44 per cent to 35 per cent but still trailed them by 17 percentage points for Westminster). This would suggest that Scottish voters will behave in line with electors in other countries that have decentralised or devolved political systems. In Catalunya, for example, the Nationalists take around 40 per cent of the votes in autonomous elections and the socialists 25 per cent. These positions are reversed in elections for the all-Spain Cortes. To add to the complication of predicting the results of the first elections, voters will have the option to divide their support between two parties under the AMS. It will not have gone unnoticed that when New Zealand moved from a first-past-the-post system to a more proportional electoral system similar to AMS, around 38 per cent of electors split their votes.

In making their political choices between parties, evidence from the Election and Referendum Studies shows that the electorate are likely to be influenced by a number of factors. There are strong expectations of the Scottish Parliament both in relation to the policies it will pursue and to its democratic effectiveness. The majority of people in Scotland are optimistic that the Scottish Parliament will give ordinary people more say in how Scotland is governed, will give Scotland a stronger voice in the United Kingdom, and will give Scotland a stronger voice in Europe. Trust in the parties to work for Scotland's interests is clearly an influential factor in explaining support for a party. Labour and the SNP score highest in this regard, with the Conservative Party doing particularly badly. Attitudes to Scottish independence also separate the voters and will become one of the main issues in Scottish politics.

As to the longer term outcome, it is harder to judge. However, supporters of independence can have it both ways. If they play a constructive role in the Parliament and it is seen to meet the expectations of people in Scotland then they can gain credit on the grounds that Scots are well able to run their own affairs. On the other hand, if the Parliament fails to make an impact on economic and social policy, then the argument can be advanced that the Parliament requires stronger powers in order to be effective. While there is not a majority in favour of independence at this stage, neither is there the strong opposition to it as expressed by some Labour and Conservative politicians.

So, there are no foregone conclusions and all the votes will count in May 1999. In this context all the parties have everything to play for. Labour can claim credit for setting up the Scottish Parliament, but the debate has now moved on to what the Parliament will deliver. Whether the plans embodied in Labour's Scotland Bill will indeed turn out to be the 'settled will of the Scottish people' is an open question. Ultimately, it is a question for the voters in Scotland to decide.

The data used in this article is drawn from the 1997 Scottish Election Survey and the Scottish Referendum Survey. A fuller account of the findings and arguments advanced are published in Alice Brown, David McCrone, Lindsay Paterson and Paula Surridge, The Scottish Electorate, *to be published by Macmillan in 1998.*

References

Brand, J., Mitchell, J. and Surridge, P. (1994), 'Will Scotland come to the aid of the party?', in A. Heath, R. Jowell and J. Curtice (eds), *Labour's Last Chance?: The 1992 Election and Beyond*, Dartmouth, Aldershot.

Brown, A., McCrone, D. and Paterson, L. (1998a), *Politics and Society in Scotland*, London, Macmillan, second edition.

Brown, A., McCrone, D., Paterson, L. and Surridge, P. (1998b), *The Scottish Electorate: the 1997 General Election and Beyond*, London, Macmillan.

Dewar D. (1998), The Scottish Parliament, *Scottish Affairs*, Special Issue: Understanding Constitutional Change, pp 4-12.

McCrone, D. (1992), *Understanding Scotland: The Sociology of a Stateless Nation*, London, Routledge.

Paterson, L. (1994), *The Autonomy of Modern Scotland*, Edinburgh, Edinburgh University Press.

Where now for Scottish autonomy?

Lindsay Paterson

The character of modern Scotland has been shaped by an indigenous civil society that has operated quite autonomously of the UK state. That autonomy, in fact, has been the main reason why the Union with England has continued to be acceptable in Scotland: a sufficient amount of domestic freedom could be combined with access to markets and cultural influences in Britain and further afield.

This old balance between Scottish civil society and the state was severely disrupted, however, by the Conservative government of Margaret Thatcher – which no longer respected the traditions of autonomy. The consequence was that, from the mid-1980s, large segments of civil society led the campaign for an elected Scottish Parliament, specifically in the Scottish Constitutional Convention. But the relationship between civil society and the Parliament will not be easy, despite the one being the midwife of the other. Despite the rhetorical claims of many campaigners for self-government, the Parliament will be in tension with the civic institutions which sponsored its birth.

The autonomy of modern Scotland

The main point about the Union was that it did not interfere with any of the institutional pillars of Scottish independence: law, education, local government, the presbyterian church (Fry 1987; Harvie 1994; Lenman 1981; Lynch 1991; McCrone 1992; Paterson 1994; Scott 1979). For most of the eighteenth century, these institutions ran the country in ways that would probably have been much the same had the Union never come about. Although this system was reformed in the nineteenth century, the changes merely reinforced tendencies that were already present. Scottish politics largely consisted of voluntary activity sponsored by local institutions, loosely overseen by a distant parliament that was mainly concerned with the Empire, diplomacy and war.

Aspects of that had changed profoundly by the middle of the twentieth century – mainly because of the growing role of the state in public affairs. But the crucial point is that the Scottish Office was no mere field office of London departments. It had a capacity to innovate in policy, to co-ordinate demands from Scottish civil society on government, and therefore to provide genuinely national leadership. Even in this era of growing state power, moreover, there remained significant scope for local auton-omy, and quangos were a source of Scottish autonomy, not straightforwardly an instrument even of Scottish Office control, far less of control from Whitehall. Unifying the whole system was the institutional structure of Scots law. Until the 1960s, moral coherence also came from the still strong culture of presbyterian Protestantism. Their leadership of Scottish opinion, together with that of the govern-ment agencies, was helped by the continuing distinctiveness of the Scottish media.

From the point of view of constitutional theory, this national autonomy had no guaranteed basis, and that fragility was to be the source of its eventual rupture in the 1980s. But, in Scotland, the expectations of autonomy had come to be regarded as rights (Cohen 1996; Hearn 1998; McCrone 1992). The Scottish institutions were taken to be the embodiment of a putative tradition of popular sovereignty which was believed to be older and more legitimate than the sovereignty of the parliament at Westminster (Mitchell 1996; Paterson 1998a).

A memory of the generally acceptable character of this system is probably the main reason why the devolution referendum in 1979 was inconclusive (52 per cent voting in favour in a turnout of 64 per cent). Most voters had grown up with the deli-cate balance between autonomy and access to the resources of the wider state, and felt it to be congenial compared to an adventure into a risky constitutional experiment.

Resistance to Margaret Thatcher

The problem for that majority was that the old ways turned out not to be avail-able after all. Margaret Thatcher's government came to power in 1979 with a hostility to civil society that was unprecedented in modern British Conservatism. Following standard tenets of New Right thinking, she regarded civil society as a conspiracy by professionals against lay people, as restricting market free-doms – without which no other freedom could be secure – and as a repository of the corporatism which had prevented both Labour and Conservative governments from modernising the British economy. So, throughout Britain, she abolished many of the most overtly corporatist of the public bodies, appointed increasing numbers of her own ideological supporters to the many committees which remained, and eroded the autonomy of local government, the universities, and other previously partly inde-pendent public institutions.

None of this was deliberately anti-Scottish. It only appeared so in Scotland because Scotland – especially the Scottish middle class – remained quite attached to corporatism, civil society, and institutional impediments to state power. So the more that the Thatcher government pursued its programme of restructuring the state, the less enthusiastic about it became those social groups in Scotland which ought to have been its natural supporters.

The reaction of Scottish civil society to Thatcherism took disparate forms. They lobbied against particular policies, used the Scottish Office itself as a way of putting discrete pressure on the government internally, and occasionally opposed government policy outright. In due course, the unsatisfactory compromises forced by this fragmented opposition brought most parts of civil society to revise their previous doubts about home rule – hence the Constitutional Convention. The ideas produced there were adopted almost unamended by the UK Labour government elected in 1997, and were emphatically endorsed by the referendum later that year.

So the policies of both the Thatcher and the Major governments turned out to be critical. From Scottish civil society emerged a set of quite radical proposals for national self-government – radical not only in the extent of the powers which were recommended for the Parliament, but also in the proposal that it should employ proportional representation, that it should contain equal numbers of men and women, and that it should conduct its business in a much more transparent, responsive and genuinely consultative manner than the UK Parliament ever had.

Tensions between the Scottish Parliament and civil society

The question now, however, is whether the alliance of civil society and parliament is likely to be maintained after the Parliament is set up. Because the Parliament has its immediate origins in the conflict between Scottish institutions and Thatcherism, it may seek legitimacy by emphasising its continuity with these institutions. The same impulse could well come from the Scottish political elite's enthusiasm for some version of civic nationalism – nationality defined by allegiance to specific institutions, rather than by ethnicity.

On the other hand, there are several good reasons to believe that the relationship will not be smooth at all. The first is that civil society developed a habit of opposition during eighteen years of Conservative rule which is not likely to be dissipated quickly. Indeed, it is already evident in various campaigns against certain aspects of the UK Labour government's policy, such as the proposal to charge tuition fees to university students. There has been no evidence that the loyalty which Scotland had shown Labour during the wilderness years would induce restraint when Labour policies prove uncongenial.

Second, this tendency to oppose instinctively will be reinforced by the extent of continuity, during the setting up of the Parliament, for almost all the other institutions of Scottish government. Insofar as the Scottish Parliament will have to act through the same executive agencies as have been used by the unreformed Union, the Parliament will find it difficult to appeal over the heads of its civil service, to civil society. The educational or health pressure groups which found the Scottish Office civil servants unhelpful under the Conservatives are unlikely to warm to these same individuals just because they are now serving a new ruler.

Third, underlying all these particular reasons for tension between civil society and the Parliament will be a change in popular attitudes towards government that Scotland shares with most European countries. Over the last three decades, the citizens of the welfare states have become more sceptical of authority, partly as a result of the effects of state welfare itself (Giddens 1994). This current of individualistic revolt first appeared across Europe on the radical left in the 1960s, but, when social democracy seemed to be incapable of responding satisfactorily, it was channelled into the rise of parties of the New Right. Although Scots were never enthusiastic about the Conservative Party, they nevertheless did welcome those policies which appeared to free individuals from the paternalistic authority of the state – e.g., buying council houses, choosing a school for their children, or buying shares. Scots also shared in the common European trend towards the eroding of traditional attitudes. Thus women in Scotland participated in the general revolution in gender roles; people acquired the personal mobility conferred by extensive car ownership; and, as everywhere, old social institutions, such as the church, suffered rapid decline.

There is no reason to believe that these trends will be reversed, and there is every reason to expect, therefore, that Scots will be as sceptical of their new parliament as citizens of many other countries are of theirs. The Parliament is likely to be seen as yet another state institution, staffed by politicians who are distanced from everyday concerns, and serviced by officers who are as much barriers to popular influence as agents of the democratic will. The attempts to change this perception are unlikely to be as successful as enthusiasts for popular participation hope. For example, even if the Parliament itself contains fairly high proportions of women, its senior civil service and its executive agencies will not, at least initially. The problem is not that the civil service trades unions are unsympathetic to gender equality: it is simply that security of job tenure precludes a rapid restructuring of senior administrative positions.

The reaction from radical campaigners for a different style of politics is likely to be a disappointment. Insofar as the new parliament seeks to encourage a more active citizenship, it will in fact provide means by which popular dissatisfaction can be articulated. Although citizenship is usually thought of in Scotland as underpinning the new parliament, a properly active citizenry will be suspicious of it as a source of potentially arbitrary power (Hall & Held 1989; Paterson 1998b).

The fourth point is that a sense of disillusion with the new parliament will be reinforced when the high levels of expectations which people have of it are inevitably disappointed. According to the Scottish Referendum Survey of 1997, between two thirds and three quarters of people expect the Parliament to improve education, the health service, social welfare and the economy, and only small minorities expect matters to get worse (Brown et al 1998). It is the strength of these feelings that explains the decisive outcome of the referendum, but no political institution could satisfy these hopes, and so tension between the Parliament and popular attitudes is inevitable.

Who will speak for radical Scotland?

The key political debate in Scotland then will be about the ownership of these popular expectations and radical doubts. If civil society continues to be able to articulate the mood of Scottish society generally, it will continue to have the legitimacy that it has had in political debates throughout the period of the Union, and that has been strengthened by its being the means by which Thatcherism was resisted in Scotland. If that happens, then the Parliament will be the alien intruder, and the myth of popular sovereignty will be expressed, in practice, as the right of civic institutions to resist parliamentary encroachments. The proposals that the Parliament will operate by agreement and consultation would tend to reinforce this by restricting it to following the consensus among the various pressure groups and institutional lobbyists.

But the Parliament will fight back by exploiting the very fact that civil society in Scotland operated as the establishment for so long. Civil society is not nearly so radical in reality as the rhetoric of anti-Thatcherism might suggest. It may have been quite effective at resisting a reforming Conservative government, but since the 1960s it has not been notably creative in public policy. In large part, the campaign for a Scottish Parliament has been an attempt to escape from the dull conformity of the life which civil society has created for Scotland within the Union (Nairn 1997, pp194-209). It would be quite plausible for radical Parliamentarians to propose that civil society is the problem, not the solution, due to its having been complicit in the unreformed Union.

In adopting this antagonistic attitude to civil society, the Parliament could take advantage of the revolution in popular attitudes towards government. This prospect would be most likely if the SNP was the largest party. The SNP could develop a Scottish and left-wing version of the successful campaign which Thatcher led in England in the 1970s and 1980s. It could then, as she did, blame the Labour-dominated civil society for the ills which beset the nation: it could portray the most powerful institutions as complacent about educational standards, defensive of professional dominance in many policy areas, and culturally parochial – only reluctant converts to ideas of gender or racial equality. An SNP administration could propose that only a strong programme of national reform could renovate the country along the lines indicated by popular expectations. It could associate itself with sympathetic international currents, although these would be European whereas Thatcher's were American. In short, a radically reforming SNP could use the Parliament to lead a crusade against the conservative civic institutions which gave it birth.

This capacity for providing national leadership would be aided by the Parliament's adoption of the most radical available interpretation of working by consensus. If it pays attention to popular views, gauged perhaps through such novel devices as deliberative polling, focus groups, electronic referenda, then it could appeal directly to the people, over the heads of the traditional exponents of popular views.

Conclusions

The relationship between the Parliament and civil society will not be the cosy consensus imagined in much of the rhetoric around the Constitutional Convention. Whichever way the conflict goes, moreover, the eventual consequence is likely to be a gradual strengthening of the Parliament's autonomy.

On the one hand, to the extent that civil society does manage to remain the leader of popular scepticism about central authority, then there will be opposition Parliamentarians in abundance who will associate themselves with that populism too. If, as still seems likely (despite opinion polls), these tensions arise because the Scottish government is dominated by a cautious Labour Party that is still tied closely to the party in England, then the source of the problems will be readily portrayed by the SNP as Scotland's not being sufficiently independent of England. The potential embodied in Scottish civil society – in its guardianship of Scottish autonomy and in its resistance to Thatcherism – will be presented by the SNP as having been frustrated by a dependent Scottish Labour Party. 'If only', the argument will be put, 'we had a more truly autonomous political process – if only the sole fount of sovereignty truly were the Scottish people – then the disappointments of the only partially realised expectations could be overcome'.

On the other hand, if the Parliament is dominated by the SNP, and itself provokes popular discontent with a complacent Scottish civic establishment, then it will have to challenge those very institutions which have maintained Scotland's distinctiveness within the Union, but have also maintained Scotland's links with the Union. Not only will that require that the Parliament gains more powers – especially in policy areas to do with redistribution of wealth, where Scottish attitudes are more left-wing than those in England (Brown *et al* 1998). It will also require that the Parliament opposes the most British elements of Scottish culture – all those middle-class professionals who have hung onto dual Scottish and British identity even as the working class has slowly lost it. This trajectory, too, will push the Parliament towards greater independence, embedded in the popular sovereignty which it will be championing.

The argument here is not intended to suggest that 'independence' is the inevitable outcome of the tensions between civil society and the new Scottish Parliament, even if the SNP does dominate. The end result cannot be predicted because the meaning of 'independence' is being transformed in the new Europe. But what seems certain is that the dynamics which are about to be set in motion mark the end of Scotland's merely autonomous role in a sovereign Britain.

References

Brown, A., McCrone, D., Paterson, L. and Surridge, P. (1998), *The Scottish Electorate: the 1997 General Election and Beyond*, London, Macmillan.

Cohen, A.P. (1996), 'Personal nationalism: a Scottish view of some rites, rights, and wrongs', *American Ethnologist*, Vol. 23, pp802-815.

Fry, M. (1987), *Patronage and Principle: a Political History of Modern Scotland*, Aberdeen, Aberdeen University Press.

Giddens, A. (1994), *Beyond Left and Right*, Cambridge, Polity.

Hall, S. and Held, D. (1989), 'Citizens and Citizenship', in S.Hall and M.Jacques (eds), *New Times*, London, Lawrence and Wishart, pp173-188.

Harvie, C. (1994), *Scotland and Nationalism: Scottish Society and Politics 1707-1994*, second edition, London, Allen Unwin.

Hearn, J. (1998), 'The Social Contract: Re-framing Scottish Nationalism', *Scottish Affairs*, No.23, Spring, pp14-26.

Lenman, B. (1981), *Integration, Enlightenment and Industrialisation: Scotland 1746-1832*, London, Edward Arnold.

Lynch, M. (1991), *Scotland: a New History*, London,Century.

McCrone, D. (1992), *Understanding Scotland: the Sociology of a Stateless Nation*, London, Routledge.

Mitchell, J. (1996), *Strategies for Self-Government*, Edinburgh, Polygon.

Nairn, T. (1997), *Faces of Nationalism*, London,Verso.

Paterson, L. (1994), *The Autonomy of Modern Scotland*, Edinburgh, Edinburgh University Press.

Paterson, L. (1998a), *A Diverse Assembly: the Debate on a Scottish Parliament*, Edinburgh, Edinburgh University Press.

Paterson, L. (1998b), 'Education, Local Government and the Scottish Parliament', *Scottish Educational Review*, forthcoming.

Scott, P.H. (1979), *1707: the Union of Scotland and England*, Edinburgh, Chambers.

The managed break-down of Britain

Tom Nairn

In 1977 I published a book called *The Break-up of Britain*. Eric Hobsbawm turned up to the launch reception and said (and subsequently wrote) that he thought I was 'painting nationalism red'. Twenty-one years on, a version of nationalism looking a good deal lefter and pinker than the Labour Party may soon be in power in a revived Scottish Parliament.

Admittedly, in 1977 it was not understood just what 'break-up' could mean. I regret that title now, but hold the Cold War partly responsible. Its influence deformed and limited the general understanding of nationalism, as well as many national movements themselves – notably over Central and Eastern Europe. There, the absence of even minimal democracy fostered some examples of chaotic disintegration, wrongly ascribed to the influence of nationality politics as such. But it now seems unlikely that Great Britain will face any development of that kind. Its democracy remains anachronistic and deficitary, yet not to be confused with the world's dwindling band of military and one-party dictatorships. The recent installation of a workable system in Northern Ireland means that we are (mercifully) unlikely to be facing 'break-up' in that original sense. I suspect that what we may be confronting is something more like a half-managed break-down of the former state.

Avoiding pandemonium

The Irish question has been in the limelight since Blair came into office. It has brought about a formal rewriting of the Irish Constitution and a somewhat crab-like redefinition of the British one, naturally informal and only half-confessed. However, the most important part of the New-British managerial problem remains that of its relationship with Scotland. It is here that a larger and more avowed redefinition is due – with the archipelago's largest national minority, the one which historically played the most prominent part in Union, Empire and their aftermath. The Treaty of Union (1707) has been the main axis of 'Great Britain', although usually not acknowledged as such in England. It has been confidently smuggled into the new Scotland Bill on the assumption that nothing likely to happen in Edinburgh can affect it, or the overall future of the United Kingdom.

I think that assumption is mistaken. There are at least two reasons for thinking differently, neither of them especially related to Scottish nationalism (though this will, of course, have its influence as well). The first is to do with the character of the United Kingdom state. After the depredations of Thatcherism and the ascent of Blairism, we know a bit more about the old contraption: it is in a bad way. It was a gentlemanly device, now struggling to keep going without gentlemen – it does so and that's that. It cannot be replaced by well-meaning individuals, cute tricks, public relations and New Labour's steam-roller alignment-rhetoric of youth, rebirth, and everyone trusting everyone else.

The second reason is that the UK state isn't just running down, it *looks* as if it is running down. No grinding academic analyses are now needed to make the point. As one of the government's own thinking outfits put it last year, the prestige of 'Britishness' is generally low and falling, and as a trade-mark it is now a liability (Leonard 1997). There has been a fairly precipitous, and presumably irreversible, decline in the status of United Kingdom multi-national identity. You don't need to be Scottish, Welsh, Irish or any other sort of foreign to think so: the English think so too (Lindsay 1998). When authority takes to coining insane slogans like 'Cool Britannia' no genius is required to feel something may be up, and wrong. Maudlin tales about 'restoring belief in Britain' tell their own unwitting story, particularly when accompanied by hazy and unspecific recipes for resurrection.

However, scepticism about Lazarus-Britain need not imply visions of doom and disaster. Instead, I suspect we may see a fairly controlled slide towards an odd state of affairs which in Scotland could be provisionally called 'de facto independence'. Her Majesty's governments of the next decade or so will half-manage this switch, naturally without avowing it. They are most likely to continue saying (as they are doing now about the Northern Ireland Peace Agreement) that the United Kingdom's sovereignty emerges unaffected, is stronger than ever, etc. Although the new Northern Irish régime may be unlikely to break with these pieties (which console its majority), the situation of the Scottish Parliament will be quite different. Its interest will lie in extending its powers, cautiously or rashly. This is an odd-sounding creature, agreed. But is it any odder than the United Kingdom of Great Britain? Is it really any stranger than that genetically-modified hybrid which we found shyly surfacing in the Peace Agreement: 'the British-Irish Council' (including Jersey and the Isle of Man)?

The comparison with Spain

A comparative context is always helpful for this kind of debate. The one I would propose here is with post-Franco Spain. All the more so since it has become pretty common, indeed almost obligatory. Last year President Jordí Pujol of

Catalonia was amongst us. He used to come here with his family on holidays, but is now invited by the Scottish Office. The aim of his tour was to suggest that Scotland can follow the trouble-free example of Catalonia. Around the time of the visit Pujol was forcing the incumbent Prime Minister of Spain, José Aznar, into an excruciating political arm-lock in order to extract a 100 per cent increase in the Catalan share of the tax take. But let such details pass for the moment, the general idea was what counted. Donald Dewar then went out to Barcelona and did the same thing in reverse, returning thoroughly satisfied with the same general idea: here was an example of stable Home Rule contented within, and indeed fortifying, the Spanish Union.

Just what is being compared with what here? The general notion is that devolved power can quite well both co-exist inside a pluri-ethnic state and manifest an identity that keeps its inhabitants happy. But the trouble is that all the particular notions are, as between Spain and Great Britain, so utterly different. In fact they are not just different but, I would maintain, of contrary constitutional species, and visibly following opposed laws of motion.

From 1975 to 1978-9, there took place a long process designed to 'establish a legal framework for the emergence of parliamentary democracy' (see Heywood 1996). From the start there was a recognition that this framework had to encompass the various national and quasi-national populations of Spain, especially the Basque Country and Catalonia. It was constructed around the famous Article 2:

> The Constitution is based on the indivisible unity of the Spanish Nation, common and indivisible fatherland (patria) of all Spaniards. It acknowledges and guarantees the right to autonomy of the nationalities and regions which form it and the solidarity among them (Conversi 1998).

That was a contradiction, of course – but recognised as such. The main point of the new Constitution was to resolve the contradiction, or at least make it tolerable; and the way to do this was a central apparatus capable of legislating for variety and subsequent change or evolution. For example, a Constitutional Tribunal was established (Clause IX) and placed above both the executive and the normal judiciary – capable of passing judgement on the Central government as well as on the Autonomous Communities. Separate from the Supreme Court, this tribunal also has seventeen different High Courts under it, created to oversee the legislation of the communities themselves.

Thus a formidable set of hydraulic works were put in place, as part of an overall new, modernised, all-Spanish constitution. The latter's aim was workable democracy, and guarantees against farther lapses into civil war and dictatorship. This was not a question of Franquismo alone. Too much of Iberia's previous history had been one of failing empire and faltering or distorted modernisation, and there was a fundamental resolve to break decisively with that sort of Hispanidad. Thus the Catalans, Basques, Galicians and other nationality groups or distinct regions benefited from the profoundest possible tide of general renewal. They went along with it because it was so manifestly in their separate interests to do so. But the main motor of change was not in the periphery – a periphery, we should remember, far more significant for Spanish development than that of the British Isles has ever been. The catalyst lay in Castilla, Aragón and Andalucía themselves, within the core of the old empire. Its source was shame, dread of backwardness, and hatred of dictatorial barbarism.

Hydraulics vs. sandbags

The new all-Spanish constitution is a great success story. Heywood's account shows what enormous efforts it required to set up and start working. The success has been neither instant nor total. Conversi's complementary study of peripheral nationalism makes clear the new problems it also created, and (above all) the limits to its working imposed by conditions in the Basque Country. But from our angle today, these very failings may help to underline the principal point: even this degree of success demanded a constitutional revolution to get anywhere. The somewhat grandiloquent structures of New-Spanish constitutionalism can in that sense be compared to major works of hydraulic engineering, complete with central dams, re-routed rivers, canals, barrages and overflows. Its fundamental purpose was control and correlation of the resources of national identity in the peninsula, including those of the central tableland and the former latifundist South and West.

In passing, it is important to mention these are not the sole such works on the post-war European scene. Those of Germany and Belgium are imposing too (and used just as frequently in misleading comparisons with the UK). Those in Italy started off in similar style, but succumbed to corrupt one-party centralism long before completion, then collapsed as a result. Yet here also they are, at the moment, being patiently rebuilt by Romano Prodi's government, in the hope of containing Northern dissidence. In other words, constitutional 'hydraulic works' are the norm in the European Union. Except, of course, in Britain. The Thatcher era was not simply one of changelessness at that level, but of an almost religiously willed inflexibility. The socio-economic upheavals of the period were counter-balanced (deliberately or not) by ultra-orthodox re-affirmation of a time-honoured British evolutionism: an insistence upon the absolute capacity of the existing system to meet and master all conceivable contingencies.

Quite abruptly, after 1 May last year, three important changes were promulgated in Ireland, Scotland and Wales. Though verbally presented as instalments of some wider process of reform ('a modern political system', etc), these fits of alteration have inevitably been carried out by central power without any prior changes to its own disposition. That wider process is to come later (the new electoral system, the new style House of Lords, and so on). And one must say at this stage that it is limping rather than hurtling towards us. The point is that this political sequence, as yet but dimly discernible, is virtually the contrary of the Spanish one. There may also be some points in common, like 'modernisation' and claims to strengthen democracy; but these are pretty vague.

In the mainstream constitutional and juridical terms mentioned, Spain and the United Kingdom are not truly comparable at all. What corresponds in Britain to the impressive 'hydraulic works' of the Spanish post-dictatorship state is more like a pile of hastily-assembled and already leaking sandbags. In Britain a style of essentially conservative minimalism continues to prevail, albeit enfolded by a new style of rhetoric. The prevalent assumption remains that people of good sense will be able to 'make things work'; 'things will work out'; 'things must be allowed to settle down' (and so on). In one sense these seem like truisms only a pedant could dispute; but in truth they are also reiterations of the old régime, the essence of the Crown & Parliament constitution. One might call it the 'natural channels' approach as compared to the 'hydraulic works' approach.

In the realm of the Unwritten Constitution, an unbelievable complacency continues to prevail. In reality, the deportment of the UK constitution may have changed vis-à-vis Ireland – it did so even under Thatcher and Major. But such inflexions have made no substantial impact on deeper attitudes. One suspects the same will be true for Scotland and Wales. All that 'radicalism' implies here is recourse to another piece of fusty mythology, the notion that the British Constitution is completely flexible as well as completely and agelessly rigid. Such are the marvels of unwrittenness. Being able to adapt to anything at all, while remaining the same, there can be no reason why it should not accommodate to new power-centres in Edinburgh, Belfast and Cardiff. The only alternative (uncomfortably like the Spanish and other models) would have been to spend some years creating a new all-British constitutional system first, and then go on to set up devolved governments where needed, or demanded. There is no indication that Blair's party or government have ever thought seriously about this.

And yet what might have been possible in 1979 is no longer so in 1999, argues Norman Davies in a recent article, 'Britain is breaking up faster than you think' (*Sunday Times*, 3 June 1998). Previewing his forthcoming study *The Isles: a History*, Davies concludes that 'If the United Kingdom can reach its tercentenary in 2007, its supporters will have good reason to feel mightily pleased…'

Identity and Europe

Something else seems to follow. If the centre is to be carried forward in this broadly evolutionary sense, with some changes here and there then of course 'good will' will have to remain extremely important. We are back with the second main factor I raised earlier on – the problem of the prestige and status of Britishness. A kind of goodwill and mutuality, or acceptance, was vital to the way the Old Constitution functioned. If no new written and comprehensive instrument is to take its place, then obviously that soul or animating spirit had better be kept going too. Indeed, given that the formal, institutional contrast between the UK and Spain is so great, may it not be that this informal, spiritual or psychological side to the comparison is even more important? Blair's unremitting, high-profile moralism might appear to suggest this is indeed felt to be so.

So how do the UK and multi-national Spain compare on this more intangible level? Well, the institutional and juridical contrast has become great enough; but the contrast of identities has become devastating. Between 1977 and 1998, 'Spanish' has become a much more positive and acceptable denomination. The post-1975 reforms described earlier were meant to produce this effect too, and seem to have done so reasonably well. Spain has become a democratic society, established enough to survive both the epidemic of sleaze which overtook the Gonzalez régime, and the recent change of government. The contrast with the Hispanidad of the 1960s and earlier could scarcely be greater. The dark, claustrophobic, pride of an ex-imperial society immured from modernity has given way to emphatic, or even raucous, Europeanisation. The Catalans used to enjoy comparing themselves as 'European' in just this sense – hence naturally different from backward, militarist, theocratic and rural Castilla. But in fact, both cultures seem to have been swept forward together in the rising tide of the 1980s and 1990s.

Spain even managed to invent a new monarchy for itself over the same period. Monarchy had been cautiously restored by the heirs of the dictator in order to preserve some of the antediluvian values of Spanishness. But after the failure of the Tejero coup, this new system became genuinely popular. Juan Carlos had the sense to support democracy, instead of endorsing a slide back into the old days. This was far more than 'modernising' the institution in the tedious British sense we know only too well. We are now enduring another bout of it under the Blair-Charles régime – making the throne more user-friendly and approachable, learning the lessons of Diana, and so forth. The rejuvenation of Hispanic monarchy took place because there was a new democratic constitution in existence; it was precisely not moral window-dressing to help keep an old one going.

In Britain as a whole, what has the story been over the same period? The diametric opposite. British democracy, I think by almost universal agreement, has declined and lost prestige over the same twenty-year period. The inflexibility of the Thatcher-Major era brought into disgrace the more civic and parliamentary traditions of the old Union state, while at the same time the Union monarchy underwent the most startling and symptomatic of transformations. The main symbolic instrument of 'Britishness' sank into a kind of prolonged moral collapse – via sundry incidents which I don't need to remind people of today. This unstoppable glissade went on until the extraordinary phenomenon of Princess Diana's death, and the popular reaction to it, when it was 'stabilised' by Tony Blair and his government. Since when Labour have been striving – without much success – to rehabilitate the institution parallel with other redemption crusades like 'Cool Britannia' and Millennial Britain.

Having decided against the kind of new hydraulic-works constitution commended to them by Charter 88, Labour believes that vigorously artful touches all round – devolution, a new House of Lords, a finessed electoral system aiming at long-term coalition régimes – will somehow do the trick, in conjunction with a made-over Prince Charles.

The consolidation of democracy in Spain was also its entry into Europe. The construction of a new national identity sought a strongly European dimension from the start, and was resolved to make them compatible. This was unquestionably one key thing which made L'Estado de las nacionalidades possible. It was particularly important in Catalonia. Had post-Franco Madrid sulked about Europe, fretted upon the spoliation of sovereignty, wielded the veto power and threatened withdrawal, then (on Conversi's account, 1998) the Catalans would already have seceded. In other words, had Spain behaved like the United Kingdom over the 1980s and early 1990s, then even the hydraulic works might not have been enough to keep it intact.

Of all the powerful intangibles, this may be the most important. The Spanish Union bore all the Spanish countries into Europe. Once in, the Common Agricultural Policy had the same profoundly beneficent effect as elsewhere – it helped to draw the teeth of rural backwardness and clerical obscurantism, and hence to attenuate once and for all the ultimate sources of identity-reaction and ethnic closure. It dispelled the roots of fascism from Spain, as it was later seen to have eliminated the basis of ethno-linguistic nationalism from Ireland. Now, although Great Britain didn't literally withdraw from the European Union (indeed grudgingly went along with things like the Single European Act and then Maastricht), it did ideologically withdraw for most of the Thatcher period, and made itself chronically unpopular there. The prestige of 'Britishness' was never lower, and the fag-end of the Tory period of government was passed in a kind of anti-European stupor ('Euro-scepticism' etc) which seemed for a time to be looking forward to actual exit from Europe by a plebiscite, and to a new version of right-wing all-British identity.

The end of the tether

One general conclusion to be drawn is, surely, that these general conditions are very unlikely to be reversed. Blair's government and its obsession with newness, youth and 'radicalism' may be aiming in the right direction. But it is simultaneously avoiding the constitutional 'revolution-from-above' which alone seems capable of altering the course of state. It has indeed – though inadvertently – launched something like revolutions on the periphery, most significantly in Ireland and Scotland. But the crucial difference from the Spanish case is that it has not done so in the centre – not, that is, for the 80 per cent plus of the population represented by Great Britain's Castilla, England. On the contrary, it has notoriously done all in its power to placate and conserve the supposedly unalterable conservatism of 'Middle England'.

Thus the main motor of constitutional change remains absent from the United Kingdom, in spite of its striking devolutionary manoeuvres, and its loud rhetoric of the new. Indeed its government is presiding over a fundamental contradiction, between the forces released and encouraged on the periphery and those being contained and recycled at the centre. In Spain, the secret of post-dictatorial success was common and highly institutionalised forward motion. In Britain, we see instead a piecemeal, staggered attempt at redemption, in which different populations have been set moving in various directions with almost no restructuring of the central institutions at all – as if sheer goodwill, common sense and compromise will be enough to retain the unitary state. 'It will all settle down' – except that there is, in comparative terms, practically no new framework for anything to settle down into.

Is this not why so many in Scotland – including many in the Labour Party – have so rapidly become small-'n' nationalists? I think it is extremely unlikely that most of them have undergone 'conversion' in any traditional sense, or been smitten by the predominantly fusty rhetoric of the SNP. On the other hand, they may be acquiring a sense of the sheer implausibility of having a Scottish Parliament – which most think of as the Parliament, 'ours' as distinct from 'theirs' – trying to rule within a framework now devoid of glamour or even minimal prestige, regulated by divergent conservative norms, and moving in possibly quite different strategic directions. What I called 'de facto independence' will be little more than cognisance of that situation, whichever party or parties end up in control at Holyrood. But the situation itself is being created by the persisting dilemma of United Kingdom run-down, that atrophy and shrinkage which Blairism seeks to remedy more by incantation than by the constitutional upheaval needed in England.

If only we could be 'like Spain!' Or – in Scotland and Wales – 'like Catalonia'. Instead, I suspect that, in Scotland at any rate, a kind of independence will be thrust upon us. Because the UK state can neither back-track from such a concession, nor limit it by force, nor forever persuade everyone concerned to be 'reasonable' (i.e. to tread water), nor cut too disastrously bad a figure in the European Union, it will end up 'managing' a kind of separation of powers which looks fairly indistinguishable from statehood to most outside observers. And since the existing political world of the latter has little place for provisional, transitional, indeterminate and merely de facto entities, this kind of autonomy is more likely to turn before too long into de jure or ordinary independence than anything else.

References

Conversi, D. (1998), *The Basques, the Catalans and Spain*, London, Hurst.
Heywood, P. (1996), *Government and Politics of Spain*, London, Macmillan.

Leonard, M. (1997), *Britain* TM: *Renewing Our Identity*, London, DEMOS.

Lindsay, I. (1998), 'We're Lager Louts, Admit the English', *Scotland on Sunday*, 16 August 1998.

Scotland's vital signs:
social policy and devolution

Jim McCormick

Labour's election victory of 1997 was built on the strong perception that a change of government would be an improvement. Although the party's election campaign was driven by five key policy pledges, few supporters would insist that voters were attracted to Labour because of its clearly defined programme for government. The public voted more in hope than expectation of particular reforms. Scots voted for devolution last September in the belief that a change in the way we are governed would be better than the Westminster model. The outcome was 'less a search for policy development than an expression of political identity' (Parry 1997). This is not to argue that expectations are low as Scotland prepares to elect its new parliament. Detailed research conducted in the run-up to the referendum found that public expectations of the Parliament were a key determinant of voting intentions (Surridge et al 1998). The more benefits expected of devolution, the more likely was a Yes, Yes vote: people supported devolution because they expected it would improve the quality of public welfare in Scotland.

It is important to consider the possible developments of Scottish social policy: how should policy-makers adjust to the new environment, how might Scotland's desire to be different be expressed in practical terms? Parry's position is true as a statement of where the Parliament will begin: it is far from certain that the first election will be defined by scrutiny of competing manifestos. Nevertheless, policy-makers will have to adapt to the various forces driving support for devolution. One such force is the sense that devolution will enable Scotland to 'get away from it all', 'it' being inappropriate policy-making from London. All parties favouring constitutional change have played this card at one time or another. Labour has argued that, even with the best will in Westminster, the House of Commons cannot devote enough time to Scottish legislation to ensure that good government is maintained. It will be increasingly difficult to restrict this argument to a discussion of how British government functions. Nationalists of more than one party will not be alone in making the case for distinctive Scottish policies as an alternative to those of the Blair government. The risks for Scottish Labour are clear, and discussed further below. Before exploring the political climate in which the new parliament will work, we consider the broad social policy parameters which might be established in the early years of devolution.

Setting objectives: a Scotland index

The Scottish Parliament will face a tight public spending settlement. The potential for financial disputes between Holyrood and Westminster to undermine good relations is greater than different views about policy priorities. There are clear risks associated with the financial settlement endowed to Edinburgh. Discussions of social policy might be reduced to a defensive protection of Scotland's relative public spending advantage (Parry 1997). In contrast, if Scotland's new Parliamentarians suspected the Treasury was planning a new needs assessment there would be little incentive to take a close look at the spending priorities inherited from the Scottish Office (even though the case for an early UK-wide assessment of needs is persuasive). Holyrood can do nothing about the financial settlement in the early years. What it can do is focus on the composition of its own budget and explore how the pattern of fiscal incentives can be used to promote its broad objectives.

One way out of Labour's difficult position as the party of government is to design a distinctive government machinery in Scotland. The way government operates must be different if what it achieves is also to be distinctive (Leicester 1998). At one level, this means careful planning of the Scottish Executive with no prior assumption that Ministerial responsibilities should resemble those around the Cabinet table in London (Leicester and MacKay 1998). The pursuit of holistic government should be driven by a clear sense of objectives which will need to command the support of more than one party. Given that some of the desired reforms to the Scottish economy and society should be measured in decades rather than years, a wide consensus on these goals is necessary. There has been little practical discussion of exactly how Scotland should change in the coming years. On an institutional level, there is much talk of Scotland's distinctive systems of education, child protection and justice, law-making and local government. At a policy level, 'jobs, health and education' are the common sense priorities of voters, but their constant repetition by politicians does not always inform the debate about how to make progress in each area.

It will be impossible to know what governments have achieved across two or three terms of the Parliament unless a specific set of social policy objectives is agreed upon in the early years. A Scotland Index would help to concentrate minds on the task ahead. Designing the Index should be more than a technical exercise in choosing indicators. The Parliament should come to an agreement after deliberation about how to track Scotland's progress towards a number of broad objectives. The Parliament rather than just the Executive would thus have a sense of ownership of the Index, which should be published annually. There would certainly be different opinions about which indicators gave the most accurate measurement. The Index should equally stir arguments about the best set of policy instruments to achieve the various objectives. For example, if an extra £500 million was available to reduce the stark inequalities in health or learning within Scotland, how should it be spent to best effect? A consensus approach to setting broad objectives cannot provide an answer to these questions, nor is it intended to. These will remain to be decided by political debate. Rather, the politics of policy reform should change over time to become focused on outcomes more than outputs and inputs.

The Welfare Reform Green Paper published in April 1998 set 32 performance indicators to judge progress over the next ten years, following the Government's five key manifesto pledges. Some of these are more appropriate for Scotland than others. There will be strong pressure for 'hard' indicators like NHS waiting lists and class sizes to be prioritised. These are vital signs but they do not measure the 'pulse' of Scotland well enough to provide a thorough diagnosis. Holyrood may come to see these as important second-order indicators (or outputs). It may emphasise the outcomes of improved education and health in aggregate terms, as well as reduced inequalities in learning and well-being, as its first-order objectives. It might also choose alternative indicators of economic inclusion in addition to the benefits-to-work transition achieved through the New Deal. For example, the target of reducing long-term unemployment to close to zero could be set.

There are other indicators of civic health which would begin to provide a more accurate picture of Scottish society. Among these are parental self-esteem, the degree of trust people have in public and private bodies, and in each other, and the level of optimism individuals and households have about the future. What we think we know and what we actually know depends on what we measure.

Holistic budgets

If holistic government would be helped by an outcome-focused Scotland Index, it also requires the development of holistic budgeting. The design of the Scottish Executive should be driven by the objective of better inter-departmental working, and an acceptance of the need to engage in the more difficult task of negotiating government across a number of tiers. The case for a small number of more creative ministries, some with joint responsibilities, has been developed by Leicester and Mackay (1998). The orthodoxy of annual accounting through tightly-defined departmental budgets would need to be challenged. The goal should be to create space for innovative practice where it is most needed on a long-term basis.

In the first instance this will probably require a small number of pilot projects to demonstrate how the pattern of costs and benefits can be shared between a number of departments. Some of the most effective school-based initiatives in excluded communities involve mothers in family learning projects, or former manual workers passing on their practical skills to school children. The impact is typically measured in terms of improved literacy/numeracy and attendance/attainment rates among children. Yet the benefits for adults in terms of self-esteem, reduced depression, less isolation and improved mental well-being are tangible. There may be a strong case for sharing some of the costs (and any identifiable savings) between the health budget and the education budget. There is no shortage of partnership working at a local level, but it is unevenly developed and insecurely financed. As our awareness of how to achieve change improves, joint budgeting around small projects should come to influence the reform of mainstream spending. It is likely to mean that the line between what is statutory and what is discretionary is flexible rather than fixed.

Points of difference

Devolution campaigners have constantly stressed the right of the Parliament to debate any issue it wishes to, whether it is part of its devolved remit, reserved to Westminster or an international responsibility. Parry (1997) describes the reservation of social security powers to Westminster as 'largely unthinking' and a 'major constraint' on the Parliament's capacity. If Holyrood had been sitting last December, it would nevertheless have wished to debate cuts to lone parent benefits at the same time as Westminster. Scottish Labour would have come under pressure from the SNP and Liberal Democrats, and a number of its own MSPs, to criticise the Government's decision. One would have hoped that the debate would not have been reduced to the predictable battle between New and Old Labour. There is a credible case for retaining and improving the non means-tested One Parent Benefit on the grounds of welfare-to-work as well as anti-poverty. Such benefits can serve as a bridge into work, as the Government has recognised in raising Child Benefit. There was too little space for what might be called the 'critical moderniser' position to be aired in the House of Commons, even though it is well represented among the ranks of the Parliamentary Labour Party.

In contrast, Labour's MSPs will not owe their career prospects directly to ministers and their deputies in London. A different system of patronage will emerge. On some issues Scottish Labour will be more in tune with Westminster than is generally anticipated. But there will certainly be other issues on which the party should be guided by its own political instincts. Scottish public health will be affected by reforms in the Department of Social Security. In the early years, the leading ministers in both governments may be Labour Scots. There will be an expectation that these issues are debated in public as well as negotiated in private.

The dividing lines between devolved and reserved responsibilities are more likely to be drawn in sand than carved in stone. Changes in the balance of initiative around social security policy may take place without any legislative amendments to the Scotland Bill. Well before devolution of parts of the benefits system or the

Employment Service are realistic options, the Scottish Parliament can demonstrate its willingness to contribute to the design of better social policy. One example might be found in the area of child health and family poverty. There is growing interest in the value of indicators like the proportion of low birthweight babies. If the Social Exclusion Network in the Scottish Office wanted to map multiple disadvantage accurately, this single indicator is strongly correlated with poor health in infancy and childhood, poor attendance at school and poorer attainment. A considerable investment in health promotion programmes in disadvantaged communities has resulted in only modest reductions in smoking and the level of breast-feeding among young mothers. Additional help is needed to make the healthy choices easier, and this might involve spending more money. If low birthweight were included in the Scotland Index, as it is in California's Silicon Valley Index for example, the Parliament could explore how changes in the benefits system could help to address the problem.

One option is to start paying Child Benefit during pregnancy, since the phasing of benefit payments may be as important as their level. Random control trials in the USA have demonstrated that additional cash transfers to pregnant women living on low-incomes are associated with improved birth-weights. There is no reason why the Scottish Parliament could not negotiate a series of pilots with the DSS/Benefits Agency to test the effects of paying Child Benefit earlier in different types of neighbourhood. One pilot might involve a direct cash payment. Another might test payment of Child Benefit through the ante-natal clinic or GP's surgery, alongside practical advice on healthy eating and smoking-cessation. The money could be paid as cash or in the form of a smart card with credits for healthy food and baby clothes. Such an approach would have the advantage of yielding conclusions quickly. Pilot projects should attract additional budgets, although revenue-neutral models to test new ways of distributing the same budget are more likely.

There are other areas of reserved policy where the Scottish Parliament could experiment. Benefit take-up campaigns in low-income neighbourhoods organised by local authorities can have a significant impact on local purchasing power. Less effort has gone into claims for in-work benefits. Britain has devised a raft of bridging benefits, grants, subsidies and tax breaks for the unemployed and their prospective employers to encourage the move back to work. Yet there is growing evidence that advice about this part of the benefits system is uneven, out of date and sometimes wholly inaccurate. In addition, Incapacity Benefit claimants have few incentives to be active in case their benefit entitlement is put at risk. The 'Therapeutic Earnings' rule allows claimants to undertake small amounts of voluntary work for rehabilitation or to prevent their condition worsening. However, there is little evidence that the Benefits Agency actively promotes joint working between GPs and community sector initiatives to make use of this rule. Most of the policy levers required to raise skills and employability will be devolved. While powers over the Employment Service will be reserved, the Parliament could nevertheless make significant progress by designing a more holistic network of existing employment and careers advice services. On these and similar issues, Holyrood can set targets for more effective delivery of the existing system of benefits and employment advice.

It is possible that new forms of economic ownership will emerge in Scotland before the rest of Britain. At an industry level, Scottish water and sewerage services could be transferred to mutual companies or 'consumer co-operatives'. Having avoided water privatisation when it occurred in England and Wales, the Parliament is likely to review the Scottish Office decision to retain the system of quasi-public Water Authorities. If it wishes to tackle the twin problems of insufficient capital investment and weak democratic accountability, mutualisation may offer a genuine 'third way' (which slow privatisation does not). Similar issues apply at the household level. The Parliament may set a target of raising the Scottish savings rate and conclude that the Government's Individual Savings Accounts (ISAs) are unlikely to attract low-income households. It might explore the possibility of launching a Scottish Savings Bond, perhaps using National Savings as the investment vehicle and the Post Office for distribution. The aim would be to give economic expression to Scottish political identity by providing a simple savings vehicle that could be accessed by all.

The Parliament should engage in a two-way trade of policy ideas. As well as seeking to influence British social policy, it should apply lessons from elsewhere when appropriate. Holyrood is likely to pride itself on establishing stronger links with Ireland, Scandinavia and the rest of the EU; so much is uncontroversial. The real test of political maturity will turn on whether Scotland commits itself to keeping the lines of communication with the rest of Britain open. A promising example is Glasgow's Employment Zone, one of only five prototype initiatives across Britain. It owes more to the DfEE and Glasgow Development Agency than the Scottish Office. There is a strong element of networking between the Employment Zones. Scotland will be in a position to learn from the rest of Britain only if it wishes to rather than because it is forced to.

A climate for policy innovation?

I t is unclear how soon Scotland can develop a distinctive policy agenda. The elections in 1999 will be driven by personal leadership (Dewar vs. Salmond) and arguments about which is 'the best party for Scotland' in broad terms rather than around the detail of policy reform.

Labour will argue that Scotland's interests are best represented by a Scottish Chancellor holding the purse-strings. Budget increases planned through the Comprehensive Spending Review will be contrasted with the SNP's proposals. The party will stick to its core issues of 'jobs, health and education'. It will hope that this strategy will attract back the swing group of 'Salmond-Labour' voters (between one fifth and one quarter of Labour supporters who intend to vote SNP in 1999 according to *The Herald*'s System Three polls). Given the scale of the swing to the SNP from the Conservatives since 1992, Scottish Labour will be in the unusual position of hoping for a modest Tory recovery to halt the SNP's progress.

'Made in Middle England' is a damaging charge that the 'Union-State' parties will wish to avoid; each will compete to demonstrate that their manifestos are 'Made in Scotland'. While the Liberal Democrats have developed quasi-federal policy making structures and the Conservatives have moved to establish policy machinery distinct from the UK party, Labour faces a tougher challenge. The party contested the elections of the 1980s as the best party to defend Scotland against Thatcherism. 'Scottishness' was deployed as a defence mechanism against an intransigent Westminster government. Devolution means politics cannot continue as business as usual, regardless of how well the UK Government is perceived to be performing among Scots.

Scottish Labour has realised that it cannot expect an electoral dividend next May for having secured the Parliament. It is not clear that voters – including many who are prepared to back Tony Blair at the next UK election – will wish to elect a Labour government in Scotland when one exists in London, unless the 'added value' of devolution can be explained in practical terms. The 'Time for a Change' sentiment has not been satisfied in Scotland. The view that the Scottish Office 'hit the ground strolling' prompted unflattering comparisons with Downing Street and Whitehall.

The problem facing the SNP is rather different. Seeking to form a coalition government in the first term, it will have to draw up a manifesto for devolved government, when all of its machinery has been geared up for independence. Publishing two manifestos simultaneously would demonstrate the limits of devolution (and thus play to the party's strengths), but it will also highlight the limitations on its own capacity to be different. Holyrood cannot cancel Trident and use the savings for pensions and housing.

With the 'old Union' buried before the Scottish Parliament has been elected, the constitutional question will focus entirely on the merits of devolution vs. independence. One scenario is that devolved government proves so successful that the Scots decide to go further and vote to form their own state. Yet the political forces for independence are usually driven by a sense of grievance which has never been resolved satisfactorily. It is less likely that satisfaction with the Scottish Parliament will prompt a decisive shift in favour of independence. A second scenario holds that the dynamics of constitutional change are driven at least as strongly by the relationship between Edinburgh and London as factors internal to Scotland, and above all the sense that Scotland gets fair treatment from London. If Whitehall and Westminster strive to make a success of partnership with devolved government, independence is less likely to be an attractive option.

There will be greater electoral competition in Scotland next year than there has been for thirty years. The politics of government and opposition exists in a way that is currently not true in England. What we might call the 'difference imperative' will strongly influence election rhetoric, but the substantive social policy agenda of each party will be slower to adapt. Following Paterson (1997), the scope for policy diversity in the quasi-federal state, which Britain will become, lies as much in the detailed implementation of legislation as in determining its broad sweep. Distinctive social policy in Scotland is more likely to flow from how the machinery of government is designed than how the block grant can be augmented using the Parliament's modest tax-varying powers. Fitting government for this purpose may not provide any obvious electoral advantage, but it could offer a more secure route to making devolution work.

References

Leicester G. (1998), 'Scotland: How to be Different', *Renewal*, Vol. 6 No. 1, London, Lawrence & Wishart, pp 65-73.

Leicester G. and MacKay P. (1998), *Holistic Governments: Options for a Devolved Scotland*, Edinburgh, Scottish Council Foundation.

Parry, R. (1998), 'The Scottish Parliament and Social Policy', *Scottish Affairs*, No.20, Summer, pp 34-46.

Paterson, L. (1997), 'Scottish Autonomy and the Future of the Welfare State', *Scottish Affairs*, No.19, Spring, pp 55-73.

Surridge, P., Paterson, L., Brown, A. and McCrone, D. (1998), 'The Scottish Electorate and the Scottish Parliament', *Scottish Affairs*, Special Issue: Understanding Constitutional Change, pp 38-60.

The bulldogs that didn't bark . . . or whatever happened to England?

Iain MacWhirter

This autumn a remarkable thing will happen – though hardly anyone will notice. The Scotland Act will arrive on the Statute Book intact and unremarked, with no bangs and precious few whimpers. The success of Donald Dewar's devolution bill has been so complete that the debate on it rapidly became a foregone conclusion and the media lost interest in it long since. In Scotland, home rule is history – the debate has moved on to the merits of independence.

For those of us who have followed the constitutional debate, this devolution walkover has been a surprise, to say the least, and a welcome one. No one old enough to remember the 1978 Scotland Bill – the late nights, theological disputes and endless procedural wrangles – could have been unaware of the risk that history might repeat itself. Of course, Tony Blair has a majority of 179 whereas, in 1978, Jim Callaghan ran a ramshackle minority administration dependent on Liberals and Scottish Nationalist MPs. The Labour majority however doesn't entirely explain the remarkable ease with which the Scotland Bill passed through the Commons this year.

The non-debate on devolution

Certainly, the Labour government had never expected that it would turn into such a non-event. The legislative decks were cleared for the great debate on the constitution, and when it turned into the great yawn, government business managers were wrong-footed. Of course, the massive endorsement of the Scotland White Paper in the September referendum gave it a head wind, and simultaneously took the wind out of the sails of the Conservative unionists. The Opposition constitution spokesman, Michael Ancram, began his prosecution of the bill by announcing from the dispatch box, on day one, that he saw his job as being not to oppose it, but to improve it. That was only a belated recognition of the political reality in Scotland. The last thing the Scottish Tories needed, wiped out in Europe and Westminster and with no Scottish councils, was a kamikaze raid on legislation which had been supported by three out of four Scottish voters. The Tories chose discretion over valour.

Nevertheless, the failure of the anti-devolution forces to mount any significant challenge to the Scotland Bill was curious and has never been properly explained. It was as if England had fallen off the map. Where were all the English Conservative MPs from the shires who had been warning that devolution would break up Britain; would create constitutional anomalies; and would not be tolerated by right-thinking Englishmen? The former Prime Minister, John Major, was prepared to lead the charge. Cynics might say that this alone was enough to discourage the hardiest unionist, but Major wasn't alone in his opposition to what he always called 'the most dangerous proposition ever put to the British people'. There were powerful forces in the English media which might have been expected to raise some intellectual opposition at least.

The *Daily Mail*, the *Telegraph*, the *Times*, the *Sun* and the *Express* have all been bitterly hostile to devolution at one time or another. Certainly, they turned it into a potent issue in the 1992 general election campaign, and made Neil Kinnock out to be a constitutional naff, tampering with things he didn't understand. Many of us expected the 'right-wing' press to use the occasion of the Scotland Bill to foment an English backlash, perhaps with the intention of encouraging a revolt in the House of Lords. But it was not to be. The editorials thundered not.

Paradoxically, the only publication to take the English backlash seriously, and to give extensive editorial coverage to it, was the *Scotsman*. Under its new editor-in-chief, Andrew Neil, the Edinburgh broadsheet argued strongly that, since Scotland received more per head in identifiable public expenditure, England would demand a price for a Scottish Parliament. It devoted considerable space to the attempts by English Labour MPs on the treasury select committee to force a review of Scottish public spending and the Barnett Formula. The *Scotsman* even went so far as to propose that all taxes should be raised in Scotland and a percept remitted to London for defence, foreign affairs and central administration. This fiscal nationalism might have seemed incompatible with the paper's editorial defence of the Union, but its editorial premise was that England would never accept devolution on the terms offered, and therefore it was up to unionist Scots to come up with some reasoned alternative which would be seen as more equitable down South.

In the end, England did accept devolution, on Labour's terms, and with little fuss. The Scotland Bill was almost completely ignored by the English press, and metropolitan opinion has only become interested in Scottish politics since the SNP started to overwhelm Labour in the Scottish opinion polls. The problem for the English nationalists was – as the pollster Bob Worcester of MORI put it – that devolution is an issue with 'no resonance' among English voters. The press realised that Middle England was in no mood to go to the constitutional barricades in defence of a Union which they were not convinced was under serious threat. And so, England slept through the break up of Britain.

My own view is that people south of the border were never very interested in devolution, and were prepared to let the Scots do more or less whatever they wished so long as they stopped girning. Scotland has long been regarded as a remote and difficult relative, who is always complaining, and who has to be humoured now and again. As far as Scottish public spending is concerned, most English people are prepared to let sleeping Barnetts lie. They reckon that, since Scotland has a population little more than one tenth of England's, any spending inequities – if such could be proved – would hardly make a serious impact on the nation's finances.

More positively, the English have long understood – perhaps better than many north of the Border gave them credit for – that the Scots do constitute a historic nation, and have an inalienable right to see their nationhood recognised in whatever democratic institutions they wish. The English are a tolerant people, unwilling to be led by nationalist demagogues into unreasoned confrontation. And all credit to them for it. John Major's vainglorious idea of a leading crusade in defence of the English way of life always seemed faintly absurd.

However, the quiescence of England over the Scotland Bill has left some further 'unfinished business' on the constitutional agenda. The Scotland Bill was arguably the most important piece of constitutional legislation this century, yet – deprived of the oxygen of publicity – the debates were limp and poorly attended even by Westminster standards. Legislative scrutiny amounted to a handful of MPs bickering with a bored minister. Anomalies were blindingly obvious and wilfully ignored, and not just West Lothian ones. There are questions of how Scotland would be represented in Europe; whether there should be a review of the 1978 needs assessment on which Scottish public spending is based. Why are abortion and drugs reserved to Westminster when health and criminal law are devolved to Edinburgh? Why are the numbers of Scottish MPs to be reduced from 129 to 109 within a couple of years? And what would happen if Scottish income tax were to be lowered rather than raised?

England after devolution

The greatest unaddressed question of all is what will happen to England after devolution. How will the governance of the senior partner in the UK have to change in the light of Westminster having been downsized. You might have thought that with so many amateur constitutionalists on the backbenches this issue would have produced lively and productive debates. But English Tory MPs, like Bill Cash, who did participate, seemed more concerned to have another go at

European federalism than to consider the constitutional implications of the bill for the UK.

And so – historians will record – the British state was fundamentally altered in 1998, as if by accident. It was a quiet revolution, if not a glorious one. Did the MPs who went off for summer recess in August appreciate that they'd just attended the last session of a truly sovereign Westminster Parliament? Parliamentary sovereignty exists now only in constitutional theory; the reality is a de facto federalism. When the Commons rises next year, Westminster will have a powerful rival parliament in Edinburgh, and infant assemblies in Wales and in Northern Ireland. Constitutional pedants might argue that since Westminster remains sovereign in the last resort under the provisions of the Scotland Act, and can theoretically override any legislative act of Holyrood, that the mother parliament remains sovereign. No one should be fooled by this. In practice, sovereignty – the power to make laws – has been divided; there is no longer a unitary state, still less a unitary parliament, in anything other than constitutional fiction.

Unlike many of his colleagues, Malcolm Rifkind, the former Tory Scottish Secretary, believes this to be, on the whole, a good thing, one very much in keeping with the pragmatic incrementalism of British constitutional practice – what others might call 'muddling through'. Though he does warn that it would be sensible to address some of the anomalies sooner rather than later – if only to avoid unnecessary constitutional friction down the line – Rifkind is right, and not for the first time. However, the problem in an anti-intellectual political culture is getting anyone to take such constitutional issues seriously. The British MP does not like abstractions, and is irritated by hypothetical situations.

The Prime Minister, the author of the constitutional revolution, has shown virtually no interest in his handiwork, even though it will probably assure him his place in history. Tony Blair has never been a constitutionalist, and was happy to hand the 'unfinished business' of devolution over to the Scots – the Scottish Secretary, Donald Dewar, and the Lord Chancellor, Derry Irvine. Fair enough; the manifesto promised a Scottish Parliament, and the PM delivered it. The manifesto never said anything about federalism. But the problem is that devolution is not just a Scottish development but one with profound consequences for the United Kingdom as a whole.

The hollowing out of the British state

The British state has been 'hollowed out' by the emergence of legislatures in Scotland, Wales and Northern Ireland, but no coherent thought has been given to what fills the gap in the middle left by England. English MPs, if they think about it at all, assume that things will go on more or less as they do now: England and the UK will be the same thing, occupying the same constitutional space; but they emphatically will not be the same thing. Once there is a law-making parliament in Edinburgh, there will be a powerful gravitational pull north. Not only will Holyrood be demanding more powers, it will expect to be accorded full status as a national legislature.

The BBC has already been trying to come to terms with this: Scottish viewers of national news bulletins are likely to become increasingly restive at items referring to controversies in the Westminster Parliament that no longer concern them. Now, of course, Westminster will still have responsibility for defence, foreign affairs, macroeconomic policy and the like. Scots will still be interested in what is happening there and what happens in Holyrood. Health, education, local government, arts, sport, law and order are all – with a few reservations – to be devolved to Edinburgh. Since these constitute much of the day-to-day subject matter of news, people will expect to see and hear them on BBC news bulletins; they will not take kindly to seeing items about English hospital waiting lists or A- level pass rates.

It could be said that, in the past, there was separate legislation for these matters in Westminster, and the Scots didn't seem too upset at their not being given prominence on national news bulletins. This ignores the 'parliament' effect. Before the Scotland Act, the constitutional separateness of Scotland was obscure, lost in arcane conventions and practices of the Palace of Westminster. In future, there will be a separately elected parliament in Holyrood devoted to precisely those matters which were in the past obscured by the doctrine of the unitary parliament. This will force the English question onto the national agenda. It will soon be impossible to retain the convenient fiction that 'England' and 'the UK' are one and the same thing. In Westminster, even before any West Lothian anomalies apply, there will be a curious sense that something is 'missing' from the institutions of the central state. The hole caused by the draining of power from the centre will become larger by the year, as the new subordinate legislatures start to gain confidence and explore the limits of their powers. Westminster will no longer be master of all she surveys. Large parts of Britain will become 'another country', increasingly autonomous and unconcerned by the passions generated at the centre.

The most visible side effect of this will be the functional redundancy of many Scottish, Welsh and Northern Irish MPs. Even though it is planned to reduce their numbers, it is not at all clear what the remainder will continue to do in Westminster for their forty-four thousand a year. Of course, politicians are past masters at finding things to do, and we can be sure that they will not be seen hanging around Westminster street corners kicking tin cans. But most of their constituents will look increasingly to members of the Scottish Parliament to address their grievances, since it is they who will be making decisions on the issues that affect ordinary people's lives.

The presence of the redundant Scottish MPs will be at first a curiosity in Westminster and then a source of irritation. They will be drafted onto lots of committees, of course, to do this and that – but their anomalous condition will be impossible to disguise. It will be increasingly difficult for a Scot to occupy many ministerial posts – not because there is any constitutional bar to them doing so, but simply because it would cause resentment for a Scot to be seen to dictate English education or health policy.

Of course, in countries with a proper separation of powers, like America or Canada, there is no problem. Constitutional roles are clearly defined, legislators know what they are supposed to do, and such questions need never arise. In Westminster though, legislative life will increasingly become a muddle, with irksome Scots seen to be meddling in what will increasingly become a chamber devoted to exclusively English affairs. This is because there is no clear constitutional place in Westminster that is, forever, England.

Eventually, the West Lothian anomaly will begin to impinge. A hung parliament may seem a pretty remote prospect at present, but it would only take a recession and a botched entry to EMU to turn the volatile British electorate against the Labour government. Before we know it, a situation could arise in which a minority Labour administration was once again dependent on Scottish votes to get its legislation through the Commons. Then the abstract question posed by Tam Dalyell all those years ago, would become a very real one. The backlash so long forecast would become a reality if, for example, English education policy were to be decided by Scottish MPs in Westminster, when English MPs had no reciprocal say in Scottish education.

There will be calls at some point in the future for an exclusively English forum to be created in which English MPs convene to discuss exclusively English affairs. There is already a precedent for this: the Scottish Grand Committee used to bring together all of Scotland's MPs to debate issues of concern to Scotland. And much derided it was too. The Grand Committee had no legislative function, and was lampooned as a 'toothless talking shop'. When the former Tory Scottish Secretary, Michael Forsyth, tried in 1996 to give it some powers to debate non-contentious bills, its impotence was made all the more apparent, because nothing important had to be referred up to the Commons.

The Scottish Grand Committee was seen as an insult in Scotland, and no substitute for home rule. It would be similarly regarded in England, unless some way could be found to give it true legislative powers. In the past, this would have been seen as constitutionally impossible, since the Commons was supposed to be sovereign and indivisible. But now that this indivisibility has been breached, in practice if not in theory, then there should be no bar to a Grand Committee assuming more of the powers of a devolved parliament. If you want a definitive answer to the West Lothian Question, this is it. However, whether English opinion will agree is another matter.

There is nothing new under the constitutional sun – these questions have been exhaustively debated before, most notably in the debates over Irish Home Rule a century ago. Gladstone initially thought that there would be no problem with granting limited self-government – what we now call 'devolution' – to the Irish; the 'imperial' parliament would just continue as it had before. Eventually he changed his mind, and turned to the 'in and out' solution whereby Irish MPs would withdraw from the Commons when matters devolved to Ireland were debated. (This never saw the light of day, since the Lords blocked Irish Home Rule.) Perhaps it would be more successful this time; certainly, the existence of a Grand Committee would be a suitable platform.

There have been other solutions offered to the West Lothian Question: devolution to the English regions for one. This is already happening with the restoration of democracy to London, and the forthcoming election of a metropolitan Mayor. There is strong pressure in the North East for an assembly which will eventually have to be assuaged. However, the problem with incremental devolution to regions, as opposed to historic nations, is that beyond the obvious candidates there is little consensus about boundaries of the putative mini-assemblies. The Banham Commission into local government, which tried to establish unitary authorities throughout England in the early 1990s, discovered that it was all but impossible to get different shires to agree about which counties they belonged to. A kind of administrative regionalism exists already in the form of the English planning regions, but these have no popular legitimacy, and the idea of grafting democratic institutions onto them was abandoned by Labour two years ago.

Far better to go to the heart of the matter and reform Westminster to recognise the new constitutional status quo. The future is federal, and it is time we all woke up to it. It might seem presumptuous for a Scottish journalist – and a long time home ruler – to be lecturing the English on how they should arrange their affairs. Arguably it is better to address this question now, rather than to wait ten years until it becomes a constitutional crisis. The tolerance of the English is not inexhaustible: it is time that the English question were properly put. The sensible thing would be to establish a Royal Commission into the Constitution along the lines of the Kilbrandon Commission in the late 1960s. The difference however would be that the terms of reference of K2 would not be to recapitulate long dead debates on Scottish devolution, but specifically to examine the constitutional consequences for England.

Royal Commissions have been derided as a means by which governments try to avoid making difficult decisions. In this case, there would be a strong case for *not* making any hasty decisions. England will have to be educated into the new constitutionalism, and this learning process could best be done at one remove from day-to-day government.

What if they set up a commission and nobody came? The whole constitutional issue may prove to be of such mind-numbing complexity that no one in England wants to be bothered with the mechanics of incremental federalism. Maybe, but we are told that the emergence of the flag of St George on the football terraces is a sign of awakening English consciousness. Certainly, there appears to be a more affirmative English identity emerging. Once a Scottish Parliament is up and running next year, England may well begin to ask questions about where she stands politically in the new order. Better to start the process now, than to allow grievances to develop which could turn the constitution into a sport for hooligans.

Mutualism
The Third Way?

Stephanie Hoopes and
Ted Tapper

E ven before the Blair government assumed office there was considerable speculation as to what core values would shape the policy direction of a New
Labour government. Would it be possible to define Blairism coherently and
distinctively? Although the Government has enjoyed considerable popularity during
its first year in office, there are many commentators – including those who welcomed
the massive electoral victory of Labour – who are already less than sympathetic with
the policy record. As *The Political Quarterly* has noted, these critics see the 1997 election victory

> as confirmation that a new consensus has been established in British politics, a consensus
> created not by the centre-left but the by the radical right. The neo-liberal paradigm of the
> Thatcher years has triumphed. Labour won so overwhelmingly in 1997 only because it
> accepted Thatcherism and proposed so little radical change
>
> *(The Political Quarterly*, Oct-Dec, 1997).

No one who remains sympathetic to the New Labour government could accept
such a severe judgement, but in recent months there have been a number of serious
commentators who have argued that the Blair administration is indeed in danger of
losing its way and needs to define for itself a clear central thrust. Furthermore, these
sympathetic critics believe that this sense of direction should be constructed around
the values of mutualism. Building upon a tradition which has deep roots in British
society, the Blair government could create for itself a clear identity which offers the
nation a positive alternative to both the free market ideology and state socialism.
While this may not give the Government the radical hue that some of its more hostile
critics demand, it would give it a distinctive voice based upon a clear set of values. It
would provide the Government with the 'Third Way' that it is so evidently seeking
(Kellner 1998, 22).

The recent experience of building societies in Britain, particularly the trend to
conversion to a bank, and then its abrupt, but perhaps only temporary, end with the

1997 Nationwide vote, provides some important lessons for a government considering making mutualism the 'Third Way'. After the July 1997 Nationwide election, we
undertook, with the co-operation of the Nationwide, a survey of its membership to
discover why it had voted by a margin of three to one to re-elect to the Society's
board five of its existing members over five contenders who ran on a platform of
conversion and in all probability to forego a windfall payment of £2,000. The vote
suggests that the preconditions for sustaining mutual societies exist. We explore how
Labour might build on this.

The mutual societies arose out of the idea that individuals should band together
to help one another, and the institutions they created should be controlled by, and
run in the interest of, their membership, with the leaders elected democratically
and held accountable. It is possible to draw at least a theoretically sharp contrast
between societies organised along mutual lines and the privately run corporations
with their appointed boards of directors, shareholders with unequal voting rights
and profit-maximising ethos. These vague ingredients of mutualism suggest a
pattern of institutional behaviour with which few, and certainly no democratically
elected government, would publicly disagree. Thus, the broad ideals of mutualism
fit well with liberal democracies. It is only when we begin to translate specifics to
policy changes that mutualism becomes more meaningful, but also more contro-
versial.

Working from the practical to the theoretical, we argue that mutualism does
provide a possible framework for a unique identity for New Labour, but that it will
not be easy to put into operation. Starting with the context in which New Labour
must operate, we then consider the lessons from the experience of building societies,
particularly the watershed case of the Nationwide. Then we consider the advantages
and problems with using mutualism as the model for the 'Third Way'.

The hold of the past

The legacy of Thatcherism has a profound effect on the future possibilities for
the Government. Although there is some debate as to when the Labour Party
started the transformation process (Heffernan 1998), the electoral success of
Thatcher, coupled with her strong challenge to consensus politics, was an intrinsic
part of that process. Moreover, in the sense that the Blair government wants to create
a strong image for itself, and not to continue with the tradition of consensus politics,
it is very much in the Thatcher mould. However, although the more severe critics of
the New Labour government may argue that its policy output is a continuum of
Thatcherism, we maintain that from the outset Blair's government has operated
within well-defined parameters which, while recognising Thatcher's legacy, have also
sustained some of Labour's traditions. There has not, therefore, been a distinctive
New Labour identity, but rather it has been an amalgamation of a number of different elements, and the question now is whether these ingredients can be blended into

a coherent whole to form a distinctively new 'Third Way' encompassed by the term mutualism, rather than a pragmatic 'Middle Way'.

The main parameters within which the Government has developed its social and economic policy can be generally categorised into four broadly defined boundaries:

1) A clear rejection of state socialism and, consequently, no renationalisation, with the possibility of future privatisations. For example, despite clear dedication to integrated transport policies, there is little suggestion that the railways will be renationalised, while discussions continue about privatising the London Underground.

2) The acceptance of financial prudency. This is exemplified by Labour's continued re-iteration of its most prominent 1997 campaign pledge: no increase in direct taxation upon personal incomes and increases in public expenditure only upon the basis of economic growth.

3) A continuing commitment to a major role for the state in both the financing and provision of social goods. While there may have been a great deal of talk about 'stakeholder welfare' (Field 1996), the delivery to date has been minimal, and after Field's departure from the Government it is difficult to believe that a radical overhaul of the welfare system is imminent.

4) The acceptance of state regulation of the market. Unlike the ardent Thatcherites, it is difficult for New Labour to believe that the free market is inevitably efficient and benevolent. The consequence has been, if not an increase in the power of regulatory bodies, at least an exhortation that they need to be more mindful of consumer interests.

Although it may experiment at the margins, there is no reason to believe that the Blair government is about to abandon any of these parameters. The question for those who want to give the Government a stronger, and perhaps more radical, identity is whether within these sets of constraints the idea of mutualism can provide overall coherence to the direction of policy. Perhaps the key question is whether New Labour wants a long-term strategy for change or a new image to enhance its re-election chances.

Lessons from the Nationwide

Some argue that the Nationwide case was a unique event, while others argue that Nationwide members are either irrational or long-time co-operative ideologues. In our survey of members of Nationwide building society following the 1997 vote, instead of finding that members of the Nationwide were atypical, we found that they were rational, self-interested individuals who carefully weighed the costs and benefits, as well as the risks of both mutuality and conversion to a bank.

What made the Nationwide case different from its predecessors, such as Abbey National and Halifax, was not the altruism of Nationwide members, but the leadership and credibility of the conversion advocates. Whereas in previous cases, the move to conversion was initiated and overseen by the existing board, in the Nationwide case, the existing board opposed conversion and the case was made by a recently formed interest group, 'Members for Conversion'. In light of these circumstances and the further findings of our survey, it is clear that Nationwide members are neither unique nor unusual. Possibly most surprisingly in this respect was the finding that there was no link between party affiliation and support for mutuality in general or the Nationwide in particular. Therefore, there are many lessons that can be extrapolated from this case to the issue of mutuality on a national political level.

Our survey of the Nationwide members revealed that the most important determinants of their voting behaviour were:

- Level of commitment towards Nationwide and building societies in general
- Perception of outcomes if conversion candidates had been elected
- Level of credibility of conversion candidates
- Level of credibility of existing Director candidates
- Importance of local branches
- Importance of the existing board's view on mutuality and conversion
- Importance attached to Nationwide mailings
- Income levels and age

There are three important messages that the mutual societies can learn from these findings. Firstly, there is a strong reservoir of support for the status of mutuality amongst building society members. In fact, only 16 per cent of Nationwide members who were surveyed said that they were not committed to the principle of building societies in general. Not surprisingly, this view had a significant bearing upon voting behaviour. Interestingly older and poorer members, who would have gained most financially from conversion, were most hostile to a change of status. These were the members who appeared to have been most convinced by the mutual ethos.

Secondly, the leadership and credibility of the board directors were significant factors in voters' decisions. In this case, competent and committed leadership had an impact on voters' decisions, both directly and through the Nationwide's mailings. The higher ratings of the existing board, compared to the conversion candidates, suggests that many members looked to it for leadership. Conversely, those who saw the conversion candidates as qualified, well-prepared, committed to the Nationwide and trustworthy were more likely to vote for new board directors and conversion. Closely related was the credibility of the board candidates. Credibility was especially important to those who thought that Nationwide should convert to a bank but voted for the existing board candidates. For this small group of voters, their poor perception of the conversion candidates' credibility was the main predictor of their vote to remain a building society. Thus, where leadership and credibility were in conflict with short-term self-interest, leadership and credibility prevailed.

The result of the 1998 Nationwide elections reinforces the importance of leadership. In the 1998 ballot, members were asked to vote separately on directors and the mutual status of Nationwide. While the existing directors won comfortably, Nationwide's mutual status was supported by a narrow 51 to 49 percent margin. The 1998 election results therefore suggest that if the existing board had advocated conversion, the members would in all probability have supported the change.

Thirdly, members were rational, self-interested voters who weighed the costs and benefits of mutuality and conversion. The reasons why voters favoured the existing board and mutuality stems from their assessment of the costs of conversion as most voters perceived the windfall as credible. The most important cost was the impact on savings rates, followed by higher managers' salaries and loss of control of the building society. For those who used their local branches frequently, the perception that local branches would close following conversion was also important in their voting decision. The implication is that members were able to look beyond their immediate short-term pecuniary self-interest to broader longer term interests that also benefited their fellow members.

Thus, for the existing board of the Nationwide building society to maintain its mutual status, it needs to offer competent leadership, demonstrate that its mutual status is helping it to provide and extend a whole range of customer services that would be threatened by conversion, listen to its members, and make a consistently strong case for the mutual ethos.

There are obvious parallels here between the position of the remaining mutuals and the Government. We discuss those parallels and suggest ways in which New Labour could adopt mutualism as its 'Third Way'.

Promoting mutualism: pitfalls along the way

There are two ways in which the present government can promote mutualism: *directly* through the conduct of its own affairs and *indirectly* through the passage of legislation which would both protect existing mutually run institutions and encourage the spread of mutualism. Directly, we argue that New Labour can take advantage of the obvious support in society for a change from Thatcherism; it needs not only to sharpen its leadership abilities but to build its credibility, develop a path that is community minded but recognises the rational self-seeking side of individuals, and concede the pragmatic dimension of the task. Indirectly, New Labour can persuade other institutions to conform to its ideals even if they could not formally adopt mutual status. Although Kellner may be right in stating that 'mutualism is not an ideology' (Kellner 1998, 30), if it is going to have an impact then it has to be perceived as a coherent set of values – perhaps ideology under a different label – which is worth are worth adopting. As the Thatcher government trumpeted the virtues of free enterprise so the Blair administration, if mutualism is to be the 'Third Way', will need to promote vigorously its own core values.

The first asset New Labour has in promoting mutualism is the strong reservoir of support for the status of mutuality amongst building society members. Labour's large 1997 general election victory suggests there is also a wider pool of support, if not for anything specific then at least a pendulum swing against Thatcherism's individualism. Thus, in addition to possibly New Labour's own desire for a unique place in history, there seems to be a readiness or at least openness on the part of the British population for a move towards community and possibly mutuality.

Possibly the strongest lesson from the Nationwide's experience for New Labour is the significance not only of leadership, but also of credibility. In order to move or sustain individuals in a co-operative manner, leadership is essential. Some argue that Thatcher maintained this kind of leadership, for example, allowing her to persevere with her privatisation programme in the face of minimal public support for many of the first flotations. In order to move individuals beyond their own short-term self-interest, individuals will only be persuaded to follow leaders who have proved themselves to be credible. As the boards' high ratings in the Nationwide case were vital to swinging many members who otherwise preferred conversion, New Labour must project an image not only of leadership but also credibility if it is to lead British voters in a new, co-operative, direction. An example of the importance of credibility is the 1992 general election where opinion polls showed that voters favoured Labour on all the issues, and yet re-elected the Conservatives. One interpretation of the result is that the credibility of Neil Kinnock's prospective government made voters question whether promises would be fully kept. In other words, leadership and credibility overrode specific issue preferences.

While there is clearly support for a 'Third Way', there is no evidence that either members of the Nationwide or British society have become full fledged altruists unconcerned about their own well being. Thus, the 'Third Way' needs to take into account that individuals are rational, self-interested actors. While they may be able to look beyond their immediate short-term pecuniary self-interest with the appropriate leadership, they must be able to recognise that even the broader longer term interests benefit themselves as well as their fellow voters.

Any government, therefore, has to recognise that it will need to construct a number of balances between short-term and long-term interests, between differing inputs into the governing process, and between policies which, although within themselves all desirable, may be in conflict. For example, the occasional need for secrecy runs up against the general desire to promote open government. Alternatively, while all voters may be equal in the polling booth some issues require, justifiably, a government to lean heavily upon well-organised special interests. In addition, while job creation is to be encouraged, should it be pursued regardless of the cost – either to the taxpayer or to the environment? Finally, while citizens may dislike cronyism, hopefully only a few are so unsophisticated as to not comprehend that government appointments are based in part upon the balancing of different party interests and the rewarding of loyal service, as well as the need to ascertain individual competence for the job. In other words, governments must balance the short-term considerations, such as the desire to be re-elected, the need to hold the government together or even the political necessity of placating powerful interests, which seemingly undermine their longer term value positions, in order to survive another day so that they may ultimately be able to implement their longer term goals.

The indirect support of mutualism is far more straightforward to interpret: the Blair administration could enact a range of measures which further the interests of existing institutions run on mutual lines: by protecting them from those who wish to change their status, by removing some of the restrictions upon their business activities, and by encouraging others to assume mutual status. In fact the Government has already moved in this direction. As John Heaps, Chief Executive of Britannia building society, has remarked, 'This year's [1998] Building Society Act will assist mutuals in competing in the tough financial services marketplace, by removing most of the inhibitions on their ability to offer a wide range of products to their customers' (Heaps 1998, 97). But there is a call 'to level the playing field further' and legislation could include 'an increase in the number of individuals required to nominate a director; and an increase in the amount of money to qualify' (Heaps 1998, 97).

Of course it makes sense for governments to enact practical reforms which aid the interests they support. However, a distinction needs to be drawn between support for those ideas of which it approves, and support for institutions with government backing, for these same institutions may have aided the governing party financially. Moreover, while it may be sensible to remove restrictions upon institutions in the pursuit of their business activities, those who face increased competition may feel aggrieved. Are the mutuals seeking special privileges: no restrictions upon their business activities while retaining the benefits that accrue to them because of their status? Finally, to protect existing directors from the threat of frequent challenges from 'carpetbaggers' may make perfect sense in certain quarters (protection is needed to ensure the continuity of smooth management) but in other quarters it may appear that the incompetent are being indulged. If mutualism is to be the 'Third Way' then the Blair government could promote the cause with practical support but it needs to tread cautiously, to guard against the charge of nepotism.

Conclusion

Can mutualism become the 'Third Way' for the New Labour government? In spite of the long and honourable role that mutual societies have played in British history, it is not a term that readily conjures up any vivid images, or even trips lightly off the tongue. Of course the same could have been said about Thatcherism or privatisation in the 1980s. Maybe with sufficient exposure mutualism can acquire its own distinctive brand image. However, whatever the label, the message and the goals of mutualism provide real possibilities for New Labour.

Mutualism's rivals, such as communitarianism and stakeholding, have not taken hold. Both have been discussed and dismissed as vague and contradictory. Moreover, communitarianism and stakeholder society have no firm roots in British society from which politicians could extrapolate or with which voters could identify. The Government could also promote and enhance mutualism in other organisations, for example along the lines of the German 'Rhineland' model outlined by Will Hutton (1996). This foreign example reinforces the relevance of the long tradition of mutuals in Britain which provides a powerful image and a history of success from which Labour could not only borrow ideas but also build a credible record.

If the future of mutualism as the 'Third Way' in part depends on the continued success of the existing building societies, Labour needs to pay even closer attention to current building society legislation and the import of the regulatory changes they are making. To merely prop up building societies will not serve the purpose. More than providing indirect support to other mutual organisations, we argue that New Labour needs to directly embrace mutualism into its own institutions and policies.

There is a wide range of possibilities within the mutual umbrella of what New Labour might adopt, from a label that would create a positive image and provide a popular, if general, understanding of its policy direction, to a more far reaching directed line of policy and institutional change along the lines of equality, democracy and balance of interests. But the major lesson of our survey of the Nationwide members is that institutional leadership and credibility can make a difference.

One way of facilitating strong leadership and credibility is to build a culture of political trust, a more sophisticated political relationship between citizens and government (European Consortium for Political Research, summer 1998, pp 13-19). Such a culture could not only enable Labour to promote understanding of long-term goals, but also enable voters to integrate those goals with their own, making them more personal and agreeable.

Of course, this means that the Government would have to avoid too much short-term serving of its own interests. Although it is naive to believe that there is a universal common good, the Government has to be clear as to its values and attempt to further them as broadly and consistently as possible. If a culture of trust can be created this should provide the necessary security for voters to see beyond their own immediate short-term interests to wider community concerns in which all could prosper. In such circumstances it is to be hoped that voting preferences would coincide with the longer term goals built around mutualism rather than be determined by narrow self-interest, so enabling leaders to take actions they might fear without the threat of immediate political backlash.

Finally, both the existing mutuals and the Blair administration have difficult pasts with which to contend. Whereas the building societies have the strong precedence of other mutuals converting, their members receiving large windfalls and increased competition in the financial markets, the Blair government has the legacy of

Thatcher's free market individualistic policies which are now established in both the Whitehall machinery and the public's expectations. The findings of the Nationwide survey reveal, however, that the public is not so deeply entrenched in the past that it cannot be persuaded, with strong credible leadership, to follow the 'Third Way' to mutualism.

References

Birch, P.G. (10 July 1998), 'The Case for Incorporation', *The Financial Times.*

Emmett, S. (30 July 1988), 'Doubts Cast over Future of Mutuals' *The Times.*

European Consortium for Political Research (summer 1998), 'Social Capital and Trust', *News Circular*, Volume 9, No.3, pp 13-19.

Field, F. (1996), *Stakeholder Welfare*, London Institute of Economic Affairs.

Heaps, J. (1998), 'Modern Mutuality', *Renewal*, Volume 6, No.1, pp 96-99.

Heffernan, R. (1998), 'Labour's Transformation: A Staged Process with no Single Point of Origin', *Politics*, Volume 18, No.2, pp 101-106.

Kellner, P. (22 May 1998) 'A New "ism" for our Times', *New Statesman*, pp 30-32.

Voting in the new politics

Mary Southcott

Electoral reform is not an end in itself, it is about changing political culture. The Jenkins Commission that reports in autumn 1998 is recommending a voting system to be judged against the current system. A conclusion to be arrived at via a referendum, to let the people decide. The discussion about how we do politics need not be overshadowed by yet another esoteric debate that only involves those around Westminster, the readers of the broadsheets but not the tabloids. Politics needs to come alive for many more people and this referendum challenges us to involve them in working out how we create a relevant democracy for the future.

Democracy is a process and not an event. It could involve many more people in exploring how they want politics to change. What can we do as citizens in the context of globalisation? Is there a third way, a radical centre or a social consensus? Instead of dichotomising and choosing between alternative futures is there no way to pool our different ideas, perspectives and experience and work from the centre out? If people are to be included then how vital are freedom of information and education for democracy? How do we consult, and more important, how do we make sure people know they will be listened to? And is keeping in contact, with constant feed-back, as important as initial consultation?

Raymond Plant's ideas on a Third Way include a concept of 'moral that some of us would call legitimacy'. This can only be derived through 'a dialogue in a diverse society, it cannot be imposed from one single authoritative source.' The moves to pluralistic voting systems in devolved assemblies, the Scottish Parliament and Welsh Assembly, and even at Westminster, create deliberative assemblies. These can 'achieve a degree of value consensus, not truth and . . . this consensus will guide public policy in seeking to restore some of the kind of moral infrastructure without which society cannot be efficient or humane.'

The debates inside the deliberative assemblies will reflect more closely the conversations in wider society, and voting systems that make votes count link the action of voting with the outcome in terms of representation. When Tom Stoppard's character in *Jumpers* says 'it's not the voting that's democracy, it's the counting', he says something which most people do not think about let alone question. That the government formed may be different according to the way we add up the votes even though people vote the same way. Although after the tactical voting in the 1997 general election we know people, given the information, will adapt to make even the most outdated system achieve what they want. But boot-out-ability is not the same as representation and the system is too slow to be responsive. When the pendulum gets stuck and then swings it does not compensate for the unrepresentative nature of the period in-between.

We need to think how voting affects our democracy. Clearly voting is something we value more when we do not have it than when we do. When children reach 16, they have some adult rights but not others, and many see votes at 18 as exclusion from participation and influence. Emancipation, we all have to learn, is not just having the right to vote but making that vote give a voice to our concerns, not about everything at all times, but when it matters. Politics is about power but we do not need to attend meetings every night to sign up for some of that power. Powerlessness is not the same as apathy, it is the feeling that whatever we say or do, no one is listening. When people say they hate politics and do not trust politicians, this is a good start to a debate about democracy, one that connects people and politicians.

Changing the political institutions makes sense in a much less deferential, hierarchical world than existed when they grew up. We inherited them from the past without much attention given to bringing them up-to-date. But now, the way parliament works is being modernised. The gender balance is slowly creeping in the right direction. But the winner-takes-all attitude will remain as long as we keep the present voting system. Cooperation is not rewarded yet adversarial point scoring often is. Problem solving is difficult if each party has to be right or wrong and certain issues are too difficult to even mention. Consensus building is an approach that says we can agree about some things and agree to disagree about others but recognises that difference is natural. We all come from different experience with differing skills, knowledge and ability.

Holistic government is about recognising that society works best when all its voices are heard and listened to. Today's politics is 'put up, or shut up' oppositionalist and often mindlessly predictable to those who are not on the inside. If we want to say 'that's brilliant but have you thought of?' or 'thank you for thinking of that but what about?' this is thought of as sycophancy instead of constructive engagement in the future. Acknowledging that we have not got the answers is presented as weakness and commissions, consultation and piloting are delaying tactics at best and more often portrayed as camouflage for splits in parties. We need a politics where politicians can be honest with us without losing votes, where their role is to explain rather than defend a course of action, and bring more and more people into the conversation.

Will Hutton in the conclusion to *The State to Come* argues that: 'Democratic government is about the business of argument; initiating processes; building institutions; creating a culture; putting in place obligations to balance the privileges of the various interest groups that constitute society; delegating, as much as possible, decisions to the local arena; and building consensus for action.'

But as a society we need to think together how that can operate. If instead of 'Education Education Education', the call at the last election had been 'Democracy Democracy Democracy', we might have anticipated yawns from the voters accompanied by cynicism from the media. And yet all the decisions that are made in our name, including education, result from the political process. The argument about democracy is about how we manage our lives, our family, our school, our community, our workplace and our country.

With enhanced technology, direct democracy becomes a real possibility in a complex society in the way it has not been since Rousseau or ancient Athens. But focus groups, opinion polls and referendums are not a substitute for, but complementary to, representative and participative forms of engagement in decision-making. But this does put pressure on politics to change. If young people see more effective ways of being heard than voting in a safe seat that undermines what we call the democratic process. There needs to be something between stopping the traffic or climbing trees and tuning out of the whole political dialogue.

Since the election some of the most radical changes proposed are about decentralising the state and giving ownership of that process to the voter. The eternal battle between equality and liberty may have been replaced by a search for a politically correct fraternity, with society, community, citizenship, inclusion, involvement all making a bid. But what could be a bigger idea than democracy? In terms of the referendum on the voting system the decision needs to be taken by as many informed people as possible.

But for those who know politics needs to change but do not want to get into the minutiae of voting systems, the voting referendum will be an opportunity to discuss how we are governed. We will be able to determine what we mean by new politics and influence the way it is achieved. Many electoral reformers will be satisfied that they have been able to send material to or speak with members of the Independent Commission. Their best system may not emerge from the Commission's deliberation but if a good one does, they will be prepared to work with others to achieve reform in their opportunity of a lifetime. The process allows for cooperation rather than competition among reformers.

The reason why electoral reform has come to the top of the political agenda is not simply because those who have least stake in the current system, the Liberal Democrats, the Nationalists and Green Parties, put it there, or even that the voting referendum figured in Labour's 1997 Manifesto. It is that there has been a dawning realisation that a high proportion of votes cast under first-past-the-post (FPTP) have no practical effect. Voters may choose to use their vote to manipulate the result through tactical voting or to make a political gesture through protest voting or they might as well abstain because it has no effect.

Defenders of FPTP talk as though it were a static voting system that operates in the way it always has. But the voters in 1997 showed they are on a steep learning curve. In the 1940s and 1950s voters did not question the voting system. If they supported Labour, they voted Labour and that was that. But then the voters started to apply their intelligence to a changing situation. In hopeless seats many of them started voting tactically or abstaining. The main parties did their best to stop them, but the voters were not stupid. They could see the futility of voting for a party that came a poor third. And it did not escape their notice that the political parties, although they condemned tactical voting, engaged in tactical resourcing, moving as many helpers as they could out of safe and hopeless seats and into marginal seats.

After 1 May 1997 there are clearly many more Conservative voters without representation. Smaller parties have always shared this fate, but what is surprising is the number of people who have voted Labour all their lives and have yet to vote for a candidate who was either successful or had any chance of being successful. It is difficult to think of any electoral system that wastes so much time and money to no avail. Nearly all the resources of the national party campaigns were concentrated on five million voters, some say 70,000. Extra agents, leaders, tours, glossy leaflets, advertising hoardings, all of them were directed at 100 key seats. If some of us felt excluded, it is because we were.

Yet what kind of democracy does not value every vote for its own sake? What kind of country does not value all its citizens equally? What kind of party does not value every new supporter without checking nervously whether they live in a marginal constituency or not? Every vote ought to be nurtured and cherished in all its aspects, as an act of citizenship, as an exercise of power, however slight, as a profession of faith. Voting is about ownership of the state. It seems very careless of us to allow this right to vary so arbitrarily in its effects from one constituency to another. It seems very cavalier to palm off the many permanent minorities trapped within the voting system with the excuse that their views will be represented by like-minded people in other areas.

Now that Kent has 8 Labour MPs, we should not forget that in 1992 it had none. Electoral reformers were fond of saying that there were more Labour voters in Kent, 223,225, than in Glasgow, which then had 11 Labour MPs. It was not satisfactory that issues like the Channel Tunnel or naval dockyards or cross-channel ferries had to be articulated by northern Labour MPs or by their own Conservative MPs breaking ranks. Conservative MPs who survived the 1997 general election, and who are all called upon by Michael Ancram to rally around the FPTP flag, should ask themselves how the concerns of Conservatives voters in Scotland and Wales can be addressed when they have no representation in Westminster.

The fundamental issue at the heart of the debate about electoral reform is simple: is it plausible to hang on to a creaking, antiquated voting system that runs not only against the long-term interest of the country but against the principles of democracy and justice and equality? People deserve a system that reflects the diversity and pluralism of the new society we live in and allows all voices to be heard in every forum where decisions are made. Would the electorate trust politicians who, after a long, searching inquiry into the FPTP system and a search for a new alternative, then claimed to believe that it was still working well? Like turkeys unprepared to vote for Christmas, MPs are expected to do a simplistic projection of what would happen to them at national or local level, their party's chance of being in government and their own chance of winning. This sort of bums on seats calculation may not work under the real circumstances of change. MPs voting in the interests of democracy and not in their own vested interest would send shock waves through the disillusion and disenchantment and mistrust of politics and politicians.

Electoral reform is about democracy or it is about nothing. It is a craven argument that reformers are only interested in democratic or constitutional issues as though they had nothing to do with bread-and-butter issues. Did the Chartists not fight for the vote for the working man? Did the Suffragettes not fight for equal votes for all? Did they have to apologise to their working-class audiences for talking about democratic or constitutional issues? Of course their listeners understood that equal votes were the key to everything else and were not to be seen as an alternative to trade union rights or social legislation. To fight now for those equal votes to have an equal value in the ballot box has every bit as much relevance.

Most people subscribe to the rhetoric of one person, one vote, one value and do not wish marginal constituencies and marginal voters to have the general elections to themselves. Another fear is that boundary commissions already influence the result of the general election before any vote is cast. That relates to the growing awareness that you can win elections by distributing your vote more evenly provided the party gets a third of the vote, but by concentrating it in a particular geographical areas if you are a smaller party. Tactical voting has become endemic. We do not even know what people's first preferences are but we do know that voters do not like voting negatively and often do not have the information to make the right choice. The straitjacket needs to be removed. Elective dictatorship, domination, one party rule, is something which many democrats find offensive whether their party is in power or not. The main positive of the present system to some is that it magnifies majorities, but if that is causing the problem, it needs to be addressed.

The argument for the status quo is that we can reform Parliament and replace the hereditary peers, set up new parliaments and assemblies in Scotland, Wales, London and later in the English regions, and reform the constitution without changing the voting system. This would be like a farmer buying the latest technology in combine harvesters, but still pulling it with a cart-horse. The voting system is the part of the constitution most in need of replacement. It is an integral part of a new constitutional settlement. FPTP may have served reasonably well at one time. It may still have a nostalgic appeal for some. But, like the cart-horse, it is best left to graze in the meadow.

The debate needs to bring in those who are opposed to change, who need to suggest ways of tackling problems in the present system, just as reformers will need to anticipate problems that may arise if we change to another system. We need to find the broadest consensus for the new system if that is supported but also to ensure that if the status quo survives those who wanted change do not feel their reservations about the current system have not been listened to. One way of doing this is to start from where we are and address the biases in the current system rather than fight for our favourite system, including FPTP, and then if we do not get it, take our bat home. If we can agree on what problems arise from change and from staying where we are then we can have a grown up conversation about the long term future.

Before we know it we may be practising the new politics. The Labour Party held together on electoral reform through agreeing to set up the Plant Commission and then agreeing to the referendum. The conversation can be about what would be a good system for this country for the next century and how can it be implemented. Or if we do not want to explore systems for ourselves, allowing the Jenkins Commission to make this judgement for us and then joining in a more profound discussion about the future.

Making *votes* count is a symbol and a shorthand for ensuring that *people* count and that their voices are heard. What is not acceptable in a grown up politics is a separation of conversations. What the political elite are talking about, and the media are covering, needs to be what people outside are interested in or wanting to be addressed. So we must look at the dichotomy that was noted in the Plant reports between deliberative and legislative assemblies. Most people want the assembly that legislates to have consulted widely first. It does this best if there are people on the inside in touch with and articulating views on the outside but also providing the places of contact for consultation and listening. A constituency-MP link can provide that but not for everyone.

Raymond Plant (1996) draws attention to the distinction between moral and mechanical reformers. He says that moral reformers start from the bottom-up. Values can only be effective in politics when they are widely shared, and the task of the moral reformer is to take the long view and try to transform the values by which people live in the direction that they want to see. The mechanical reformer is top-down, believing that there might be political, social and economic strategies available that would produce the desired results, without necessarily having to transform the underlying moral culture of citizens. In the past the second may have worked but in today's world politicians need to take people with them.

In this context, *Making Votes Count* is the network that will bring together those who support change. Labour campaigners will be working alongside reformers in other parties and none. Of course the task is to give the FPTP system a decent burial but we will need to present the electorate with a vision of the future that includes a voting system that reflects their aspirations, a system that values every vote in every part of the country. It is not simply about winning or losing the referendum but how the debate is conducted. The campaign will need writers, speakers, deliverers, commitment, time, energy and most of all enthusiasm.

With the landslide election of a Labour government, no one would suspect that we may be at the end of Labour's road to electoral reform. We may be about to challenge all the assumptions about voting systems. Any party elected by a system will always be persuaded that that system is not only the best system but needs to be retained. Labour pluralists have moved beyond this vested interest thinking. It is clear that politics needs to change and changing the voting system may be the catalyst politics needs. At the end of the 20th century, a Labour government with an enormous majority delivering the process of change and the choice to the people would start the process of building trust and connecting the people and the politicians.

1945 was the time for 'We are the masters now'. From 1997 and for the new century, politicians know that they are the servants of the people. Democracy is too important to be left to politicians, but they need to join in too. We can practise it in schools and learn from one another. Trust has to be earned but politics cannot afford to write off the politicians. People, power, proportionality, pluralism and politics make a new healthy democratic cocktail with the potential to involve us all. FPTP has served the Conservatives well for a century. It served the Labour Party well in 1997. 1945 was the opportunity to create the welfare state. 1997 was and is Labour's opportunity to create the democratic state. Electoral reform is not only a touchstone of the new politics: changing the system will bury some of the arrogance of power and usher in the new dawn of democracy.

The article draws on the conclusion of Making Votes Count, *co-authored with Martin Linton MP, which contains both the history of electoral reform and statistical and critical analysis of the current system.*

References

Hutton, Will (1997), *The State to Come,* Vintage.

Plant, Raymond (1996), 'Social Democracy' in *The Ideas That Shaped Post-War Britain*, Fontana Press.

Plant, Raymond (1998), *New Labour – a Third Way?* for European Policy Forum and the Friedrich Ebert Stiftung.

Stoppard, Tom (1972), *Jumpers*, Faber and Faber.

State, business and civil society
Rules of engagement

Sue Goss

The dust is beginning to settle on the cronygate affair. No doubt there have been some hard lessons learned and some silver linings discovered. Even Derek Draper has a new career ahead. Listening to him (again) on the radio, he seemed in his natural element. No doubt he will be offered a role as a talk radio host or a pop show presenter. The Government escaped relatively unharmed. No one managed to suggest that ministers or MPs did anything wrong. No direct access was sold, and government advisors only stand accused of not seeing the lines clearly enough.

And indeed the lines have been greying. How were those political activists who worked hard for the Labour Party yet found themselves unemployed on 8 May 1997 to pay the mortgage? They liked being at the centre of gossip and the minute-by-minute hothouse of politics. Lobby companies could offer that. And for those people who do find they work nine to five for lobby companies, what happens to the political views and opinions which drove their past commitment and activities? What happens to the friendships they formed over all those years? It is hard for those who built up a discussion network such as Nexus in their spare time, and because of a genuine sense that it was a helpful contribution to the political project, to be accused of sleaze. The Government is in most cases too sensible to allow lobbyists to take advantage. Most politicians struggle to have integrity despite the temptations. Margaret Hodge was reported as being offered sponsorship for a dearly loved project – but when the sponsors asked if she might enable them to meet David Blunkett she told them to get lost.

So it seems almost bad form to rake it all up again. But *Renewal* readers (and writers) cannot afford not to reflect and learn lessons that go to the heart of our democratic project. On one reading, the cronygate affair exposes the insidious Americanisation of our politics, and the move towards the lobby culture. Thus it can be argued that what happened is no worse that what happens in the US, in Australia and elsewhere, and to hope otherwise is naive. But if this is so, there are safeguards in place in other democracies that we lack. Indeed there are some simple things that government must do if Labour's pre-election pledge to be the party of openness is to retain credibility. For example, the Government should move decisively to ensure that lobbying is better regulated. It should create a statutory register of lobbyists and their clients. Such a register should not just include commercial lobbyists, but also campaign organisations and pressure groups (including groups such as Charter 88, and the Campaign for Electoral Reform) that seek to influence the process of government policy. Registering, declaring interests, being open and accountable about the kind of access an organisation has, is one element in a more open political culture.

The business of government

Simply regulating lobbying is not enough. The problem is about access, and influence. It is true that there are a range of legitimate services that lobby companies describe when they talk about what they can do for clients, such as PR, communications and advice. But are these what the big companies are spending big money trying to buy? The truth is that money talks. Powerful commercial interests can always try to buy access, spend to know that they will be listened to, find ways to be in the right place at the right time. The United States, where 'sunshine laws' ensure open lobbying, shows us that the spending power of the big corporations ensures that their lobbyists flood the legislative process. Whatever systems are devised, the wealthy and the powerful will always seek to secure better access to government.

That is unavoidable, but we seem to have lost the political understandings that make it possible to be on our guard against the effects of the lobbying process. In the nineteenth century and much of the twentieth century we knew that the wealthy class had privileged access to government. And if government wasn't quite the executive committee of the bourgeoisie, it was the bourgeoisie that it always met at dinner, at the theatre, and at shooting parties in the country. The history of the labour movement was a history of trying to break through those cosy circles of assumption and shared experience, to ensure that people with different experiences, and different ways of seeing the world – people who lived in slums and ran out of food on Thursdays, who had no education and whose health declined in their forties – had access to power.

Many political events are now sponsored by business, many conferences and discussions are funded by business. Business has the money; other groups within civil society do not. But what does that do to the quiet assumptions we hold about hospitality, about favours? What is the impact of meeting time after time, as sponsors, as dinner partners of those businessmen who have spent money to be there? What do they expect in exchange? Roger Liddle, speaking in his own defence, was quoted as saying: 'I see a lot of business people on a regular basis. Its an important element of my responsibilities'. This is undoubtedly true, both under this government and under previous governments. It is the business of government to see many interest groups. And we know that many ministers and advisors are listening to people from many walks of life, to community and user groups, to teachers, children, to local government and to the voluntary sector. But we need a political system where the imbalances of access are obvious, seen to be problematic and where political action is taken to put that right.

Underneath some of the complacency there is a sort of argument, which, put elegantly, expansively, over a glass of claret, is beguiling, comforting, to those on the inside. It goes something like this: 'This is a listening government, so close to the people that it knows through focus groups and surveys how they think, how they feel, and is able to understand what people want. This is a new sort of democracy, more direct, so that the stuffy old formal mechanisms, like elections, members of parliament, select committees and regulatory frameworks – are no longer necessary. And of course there are old fogies who don't like that, because they are part of the old world'. This is the dangerous element at the heart of lobbygate – not where many realised that they were foolish and mistaken, but here, in the heart of the argument, where they do not. Let us take the argument in stages.

1. This is a listening government.

Well, yes. The Government is perceived by many across the spectrum of interests as open to new ideas, new ways of thinking, capable of engaging in dialogue. Some of this comes simply from the fact that ministers are more aware of the day-to-day concerns of ordinary people, they went to ordinary schools, grew up in a wide cross section of communities, are *younger* than their predecessors. There has been a barrage of formal consultation alongside the surveys and focus groups conducted informally, and local and central government are loosening up to the ideas of referendums, citizens' juries, panels, etc., to engage more effectively with local people. This is all good, and the beginnings of something that could radically change the relationship between government and civil society. But we are not there yet. And there are powerful counter-drivers. The Government is in a hurry, and there is a tendency for processes labeled as 'listening' to seem rather rushed – the governmental equivalent of the busy over-controlling executive who keeps saying 'get to the point can you' and looking pointedly at his or her watch! Many of the tensions which the Government is trying to manage are very complex, and success will not be achieved without patient and painstaking listening and several attempts at action, each one reviewed to find the learning on all sides before another attempt is tried.

Listening is a behaviour, not an event. It is possible to organise a public relations event which goes under the label of listening, but without anything actually being heard! Ministers' lives are not structured in ways that make real listening easy. And we all know that when there is little time, there are always some, those skilled in reaching us, to whom it is easy to listen. Trying to listen to the tricky ones – young people, perhaps those without resources, perhaps those without education – defeats us.

2. A listening government means a new sort of democracy.

Well no, not on its own. Because listening relies on the goodwill and commitment of those who listen. And democracies are judged by the freedom and opportunities enjoyed, as of right, by citizens.

I am a great fan of new and more inclusive methods of engagement, including surveys, focus groups, panels, citizens' juries, consensus conferences and the rest. Indeed they offer spaces for the exploration and resolution of problems that can be beyond the reach of conventional politics. They offer, if used well, ways to hear from people who have often been excluded – homeless people, people from refugee communities, single parents. They offer opportunities to extend the number of voices heard, and to make policy making more pluralistic, more open. They can enable the devolution of problem identification and decision making directly to local estates, local wards, local streets. There are emerging methods that enable the different interests and people within local communities to come together and make decisions about how to spend money and deploy resources to make their lives better. But is that how they are being used?

Many of the techniques being used are simply the conventional tools of market research – product testing. All good companies use them, and it is sensible for any political party in the modern era to test its 'political products'. It helps to guarantee that the Government stays in touch with its 'consumers' and continues to enjoy 'brand loyalty'. But it is not democracy.

3. The old forms don't matter.

Our current democratic framework is badly flawed. To argue that informal listening cannot simply substitute for formal process is not to defend the ways in which we are currently governed. Our democracy needs to be modernised. But that does not mean that we can dispense with democratic forms. There are some vital principles that form part of any democratic process.

There must be mechanisms for finding out what the Government does in our name. This is where the Freedom of Information Act is so central to a modernisation project. If we do not know what government is doing, we cannot hold it to account, and our right to approve or disapprove government actions is withdrawn.

There must be mechanisms for challenging any abuse of power by the executive, and there must be democratically-accountable bodies able to scrutinize and challenge the actions of the executive. This is where a Bill of Rights will make such a contribution to improving democracy, and where the role of MPs and of a democratically elected replacement to the House of Lords is vital.

There must be mechanisms for the collective expression of democratic will. We must be able to get rid of governments, and their appointees. Elections are an important part of that process. The electoral system may not throw up the best people, and we may not as citizens vote for the best candidates, but we cannot simply bypass the system as a consequence. We need to improve our politics. If it is to carry legitimacy, the electoral system must be fair and proportional. That is why PR is an important element in a democracy. Referendums can also be part of the democratic process, but we are right to be suspicious about how they are held, and the questions that are asked. There must be protocols governing the way they are run. We must also be able – directly or indirectly – to hold to account those that are appointed to office. A strengthened House of Commons would be better able to hold the executive, and their appointees, to account on our behalf. There could also be more direct forms of accountability.

There must be ways that minorities can be heard, and that diversity can be represented – ways that local and regional difference can be translated into local and regional policy. Here the Government is pulled two ways. It has made magnificent strides towards devolution in Wales, Scotland and Northern Ireland, and is attempting to devolve power to local authorities, but there are powerful centralising tendencies in government. The need to 'play safe' constantly undermines the scope for experiment and license. Minorities are treated as having greater legitimacy and the Government sees social exclusion as a priority. And yet, and yet, it is so hard for the Government to pay real attention to the needs and views of minority communities in the maelstrom of conflicting interests and pressures. It will take all the personal strength and integrity of our ministers to represent the interests of the most vulnerable when it would be electorally safer to sacrifice them to 'middle England'.

The openness and personability of the Prime Minister offers a dangerous temptation. It is possible for him to appeal to us above the detailed mechanisms of parliament and the executive, and say – 'trust me'. And if we do, we forget to worry about the lack of democratic checks and balances, the absence of regulation, and the decay in the rules of engagement that govern our democracy. But we need a system that can cope with human fallibility. Moments when trust exists are the very best times to explore the mechanisms needed to ensure that that trust cannot be misplaced. Government cannot ask for trust instead of audit and accountability. It earns trust through the effective working of audit and accountability.

Rules of engagement for civil society

Both government and civil society need new rules of engagement. Government at all levels needs to develop a strategy to ensure that access is fair and is seen to be fair. We need changes to parliamentary procedure to allow lobbying to take place openly within the legislative framework. This might mean changing the ways in which Parliament's committees work, to give MPs and Peers much more opportunity for pre-legislative scrutiny of draft laws. Witnesses could be called and evidence gathered from outside parliament, not only from businesses that would be affected by legislation, but also from consumer groups and campaign organisations. Government should be forced to consult representatives of consumer interests in the formulation of policy. Ministers should insist that civil servants, in drawing up lists of consultees, include representation from civil society – even if that means listening to advice that they don't want to take. Simply listening to those that agree with you is highly dangerous, any good government needs to find ways to engage with and to persuade those who have different views.

Government should build into methods of consultation the challenge and feedback that means they can readily understand and respond to diversity. They need time to digest and explore what is heard. Increasingly, government should be less in a hurry to 'decide' and more willing to create spaces in which different interests and sections of society can hear from each other, and develop a dialogue to help negotiate through sensible solutions. There does not need to be a single model, or a single policy in many of the complex areas of our lives. The processes of policy making and decision making should be open and inclusive at central, regional and local government levels. This does not mean simply sending out more consultation papers, there is already an overload of conventional consultation mechanisms – nor does it mean simply more 'ministerial tourism'. But there are opportunities, particularly if ministers and civil servants break out of their boxes, for workshops, open space events, consensus conferences, even secondments and shadowing arrangements that send civil servants to the coal face and vice versa. The Local Government White Paper opens up the prospect of doing much of this at local level, but the lessons, and the skills, can be extended. The emerging local scrutiny role offers greater local accountability – but scrutiny at national level, the independent second chamber and a Freedom of Information Act all help to secure 'rules of engagement' for government.

The good governance of our democracy is not simply a problem that we can lay at the feet of government. A vibrant participative democracy will only work if civil society as well as government carries a sense of responsibility and self discipline. Democratic behaviour, above all else, requires a willingness to forego the vigorous prosecution of a personal interest in the wider public good. It means not always doing the easy thing to get what we want, never cutting corners that might reduce the rights of others, treating all fellow citizens with courtesy and consideration. It requires respect for the views and the interests of the citizens around us, a willingness to listen and an openness to the possibility that we might learn from others. It requires a willingness to take responsibility for our actions, and a commitment to defend and preserve the system that protects our own democratic freedoms.

We do not yet expect our schools to teach these values and responsibilities. Not all parents model them. Among many vulnerable and excluded people, they are seen as a joke. But, without them, we have no democracy worth talking about. All of us, perhaps especially those of us who work for pressure groups, or consultancies, or who are seen as 'academic experts' or specialists, or who are favoured business people, or politicians, must pay attention to the rules of engagement that make our democracy work. Corrupt or careless governments undermine democratic behaviours, but so do indifferent and self interested members of society.

It is not too much to ask of business leaders that they also take seriously the obligations of good democratic behaviours. We require, in a modern democracy, that businesses take seriously their roles as corporate citizens, and exercise the self-discipline and responsibility that their corporate wealth requires. They should not expect to be taken seriously by government if they use their money and hospitality to try to buy exemptions from taxes or regulation, or to bend policy in ways that will increase their profits. In the end, it is the expectations that government and the public have of powerful organisations that will change their behaviours, not simply changing the rules.

British trade unionism's quiet revolution

Michael Allen

The theme of this year's annual meeting of the Trades Union Congress – Organising for Fairness – encapsulated the two primary priorities: to use the opportunities arising from *Fairness at Work* to recruit new members, and to promote a new workplace agenda seeking to combine equity with efficiency. The unions were able to showcase their new twin-track approach to employment relations: display a commitment to partnership with good employers; coupled with 'in-your-face' engagement with the bad, not least with those employers who resist the recruitment and recognition drives of the New Unionism. Concurrently, union leaders and Labour politicians alike used the Congress to advertise their new relationship of respectful distance – dialogue not diktat.

Every dimension of Labour's relationship with the unions has changed although some more profoundly than others. Electorally, Labour can no longer rely on trade unionists to support the party *as trade unionists*. Their organisations cannot deliver the vote although one should not underestimate the contribution of trade unions' logistical and human resources such as office space, vehicles and officials seconded to marginal seats. This also raises the issue of the tenacity and reliability of such support. However close Labour gets to business, it's difficult to imagine corporate interests operating in such a partisan and practical manner, or business's relationship to Labour transcending the predatory and self-interested. The *Guardian*'s Hugo Young recently noted, 'When the heat's on, business can hardly be relied on. Business gravitates to power, and will soon swing away again. When the bandwagon goes into reverse, what price J. Sainsbury continuing to ride it?'

Union/party relations

Financially, Labour has diversified its funding sources while remaining heavily reliant on union cash. The most significant move in this respect was the AEEU's decision to divert a hefty portion of its political fund to a new scheme for training and promoting working-class candidates within the Labour Party. The move has attracted a great deal of interest amongst other affiliated unions similarly displeased at the evident preferences shown for London-based professionals in the selection or imposition of candidates prior to the general election. Such developments could well presage a more sophisticated approach to political funding by the unions. Some have examined the US trade unions' success in promoting their agenda by being scrupulously selective about which Democrats they support.

Yet, according to the Sheffield University surveys of party members conducted by Pat Seyd and Paul Whiteley, the vast majority of party members are opposed to major change in union-party relations. Even 55 per cent of what Seyd and Whiteley characterise as 'New Labour' members disagree with the suggestion that unions should no longer be affiliated to the Labour Party, leaving them to conclude that 'there is no support around the party for breaking the affiliation link'.

In parliamentary terms, trade union representation within the Cabinet and the Parliamentary Labour Party has never been thinner. At governmental level, some unions were taken aback during the debates around *Fairness at Work* by how receptive Downing Street was to the CBI's overtures and, by contrast, how muted were the Cabinet's pro-union heavyweights. Ian McCartney remains almost alone in enjoying the unions' trust, not least because of his openness in confronting union critics upfront for whinging from the sidelines rather than exploiting the new climate to rebuild their organisations. But many in the unions reserve particular scorn for senior party figures who have converted a naive belief in the unions as the vanguard of the working class – what C Wright Mills called the 'labour metaphysic' – into an equally utopian faith in the virtues of business and, more disturbingly, the catechisms of management gurus.

Nevertheless, New Labour does appear to have belatedly recognised the genuine sea-change in British trade unionism. Tony Blair's failure to do so at least year's Congress – allied to his condescending tone – had caused exasperation rather than resentment. This year, Peter Mandelson explicitly stated that he 'recognise[d] that the trades unions have already made huge efforts over the years to change and modernise ... [and] that in many companies industrial relations have been transformed from the old-style battlefield of "them and us" to the new-style of co-operation in achieving shared success.'

Mandelson's insistence that 'modernisation and transformation must go further' will be welcomed by many in the unions, but he understates the genuine constraints on organisational innovation in democratic organisations. Many unions would love to replace the annual conference with a biennial (or even more intermittent) event. The TUC's annual congress pays for itself by providing a shop window for the unions. For most affiliates, the annual conference is a costly affair of dubious democratic worth. But try convincing the activists to forgo their annual week at the seaside.

Few union leaders enjoy the executive powers of their political counterparts, or the electoral imperative which allowed the Labour Party to initiate such profound constitutional changes. The TUC itself lacks the authority or prerogatives that would allow it to steer the labour movement more strategically or to impose a more rational order within the labour movement. Whereas the Australian TUC was able to instruct its affiliates to merge on sectoral lines by a specific deadline, the TUC must contend with a more pluralist set-up in which some of the major unions already feel the TUC can get a little too big for its boots.

Changing the organisation

Nevertheless, many unions have followed the TUC's lead in modernising their organisations. It is fair to say that the unions are increasingly innovative in reforming their structures, business-like in the management of resources and imaginative in balancing the demands of organisational efficiency and democratic accountability. Unions are taking a leaf from management's book and adapting 'best practice' techniques and processes for the more effective management – and targeting – of unions' financial and human resources. The evidence suggests that British trade unions have begun to marry innovation to the resilience that saw them (albeit battered and bruised) through the travails of Thatcherism.

Taking a cue from business, unions are delayering traditional structures – taking out tiers of management and union organisation – to effect costs savings, decentralise resources. They are bringing the organisations closer to members. Some, like the engineers and electricians' AEEU, have replaced full-time executives with lay committees. Unison's strategic review employs aspects of 'business process re-engineering' to cost activities and benchmark good practice. Others, like general union GMB, the professionals' MSF, and finance union UNiFi, among others, have used structural reform to divert resources previously spent servicing committees to recruitment drives. The GPMU print union has abolished its regional structures and converted regional officers into organisers.

Decentralisation of bargaining and privatisation have led unions to devolve resources to local or regional level. Some have rationalised structures to bring the union closer to members using focus groups or branch development plans. Financially, the majority of British unions remain dangerously dependent on subscriptions income, lacking the pension fund and real estate assets which subsidise US unions or the institutional subsidies of their continental European counterparts.

Recognising that commitment is no compensation for lack of competence, many unions are using the union officials' NVQ, improved recruitment and selection procedures and Investors In People (IIP) to improve staff motivation and performance. TUC general secretary John Monks concedes that IIP was 'very hard work' but helped the TUC develop a 'get-on-with-it culture'. The TUC's organisational overhaul not only proved a catalyst for similar reviews amongst TUC affiliated unions but both pre-empted and informed Labour's modernisation. At the prompting of Tom Sawyer, one of the General Council participants as UNISON's deputy general secretary, members of Labour's National Executive went through the Cranfield process a couple of years after the TUC.

Such initiatives cast doubt on the caricature of unions as bureaucracies remote from members and nostalgic for the past. On the contrary, unions have been modernising their structures, management processes and policies in a little-noticed quiet revolution. The unions have survived eighteen years of Conservative governments and several pieces of explicitly anti-union legislation, against a backdrop of adverse social and economic trends. The defensive consolidation represented by the mergers of the 1980s maintained the unions' fabric. But they are now committing substantial resources and some imagination to redefining their organisations, structures and operations to reflect the demands of the modern workplace, to meet members' changing needs and to forge new relationships with employers.

The suggestion that *Fairness at Work* will prompt aggressive union recruitment drives, jeopardising the TUC's partnership approach with an upsurge of industrial militancy, is clearly far-fetched. Of course, there are still union activists who remain adversarial, fighting an ersatz class struggle – often from the comfort of the senior common room or municipal canteen. And there remain those commentators, such as Seumas Milne, for whom any hint of a strike suggests evidence of incipient industrial militancy (*Guardian*, 18 September). But the truth is that there is no serious trade union left with a viable alternative to the partnership agenda. Arthur Scargill's speech to TUC Congress was greeted with amused condescension. Rarely can a public figure have moved so swiftly from pomposity to bathos. The broad left groupings in the major unions have either degenerated into transparent fronts for Trostskyist sects (as in Unison) or represent little more than factional vehicles for aspirants to senior office.

Nevertheless, partnership does not entail passivity. The unions' mutual-gains approach to good employers is compatible with energetic engagement with the bad. But far from prompting regressive syndicalist opposition to the TUC's partnership approach, *Fairness at Work* is more of a challenge to that large swathe of employers reliant on authoritarian management-by-diktat. The real danger of reviving adversarial attitudes is that the intensive lobbying by employers' interests might lead to major changes to the *Fairness at Work* legislation and raise further obstacles to a level playing field for union recruitment. The experience of the United States certification process under the National Labor Relations Board proves that unscrupulous employers will not only exploit loopholes but systematically violate legal regulations to avoid union recognition. Establishing thresholds and, in effect, inviting a mini-election campaign around unionisation creates a highly-charged, polarised climate which can adversely affect morale and long-term labour-management relations whoever 'wins'.

The vociferousness with which business has lobbied against the fairly anaemic proposals in *Fairness at Work* is itself a disturbing indication that outdated adversarialism has not quite been purged from British employment relations – at least on the employers' side. If the Institute of Personnel and Development are correct in claiming that unions and collective bargaining are 'withering on the vine', why the visceral hostility to such a modest proposal to provide basic rights enjoyed by employees in virtually every other advanced economy?

While many unions have undertaken a genuine strategic shift towards a mutual-gains partnership approach to employment relations, it is disquieting that some employers consider it legitimate to deny recognition even when it is the demonstrable wish of the majority of employees. This de facto disenfranchisement sits uneasily with the rhetoric of empowerment. Similarly, the claim that compulsory recognition is alien to our voluntary tradition lacks credibility from employers all too reluctant to defend voluntarism in the face of several anti-union legislative interventions since 1980.

For the most part, trade unions still face declining membership although it would be wrong to understate their remarkable resilience in the face of adverse trends. The circling of the wagons seen in the mergers of the 1980s helped maintained the unions' fabric. It remains to be seen whether the organisational innovations of the 1990s, allied to the new opportunities afforded by *Fairness at Work*, will release the resources and energies required for unions to go for growth and fashion a new unionism for a new century.

Reviews

■John Grieve Smith
The Age of Insecurity, Larry Elliott
and Dan Atkinson (Verso, 1998)

In this stimulating and highly readable attack on current orthodoxies, Larry Elliott and Dan Atkinson (both of the *Guardian*) lambast the combination of laissez-faire economics and social authoritarianism which they see as underlying much of today's centre-left thinking. Their theme is that 'we need social and economic justice, that it can be delivered, and that those that currently prevent us from having it include false friends as well as sworn enemies'. The new world order is dominated by financial and big business interests with increasing insecurity for the ordinary man and woman. It is capital that needs to be controlled not our social behaviour. The new market economy has failed to meet its promise to deliver 'dynamic stability'. In the authors' words, 'From the twisted social wreck, we must, with all the stoicism of a veteran driving examiner, inform the new economic system, with regret, that it has not passed the test'.

The business ethos

Their political analysis is interwoven with a fascinating survey of cultural trends since World War Two, based on a variety of examples from film, popular television series and books. The triumph of business values and ethos is demonstrated by the way that social-welfare organisations justify themselves in business terms. They analyse the business ethos as originating from the idea that markets are the external reality against which all human activity can be judged. Human actions made in conformity with this reality are likely to prove more fruitful than those made in defiance or ignorance of it. Hence the structures and values of large-scale business organisations are applicable to almost all human organisations. So it is assumed that the management of universities, schools and hospitals, for example, should ape that of business, as the spread of inappropriate terms like 'market' and 'customer' vividly illustrates. But anyone who has had experience in both worlds will know very well that the problems are generally very different.

Similarly, political institutions are increasingly expected to mirror business organisations. Executive members, whether Cabinet ministers or political appointees, are expected to be 'undogmatic' and to prize technique and 'results' above all else. They should act swiftly with 'unfettered discretion', tying up constitutional and legal niceties later. As with business, the political executives like to close deals (as for example Tony Blair's agreement with British Telecom to 'wire' all schools free of charge in return for greater commercial freedom); they are reluctant to rule anything out on grounds of principle. Under New

Labour, legislators are now treated as the executive's workforce. Following a corporate format, MPs are expected to be the salespeople for whatever policies the Cabinet (or Prime Minister) may produce; rather than a check on its activities.

In attacking the 'business ethos', however, the authors do not make the important distinction between industry and finance. Although chairmen of large firms from either sphere are *persona grata* with the present government, it would be wrong to suggest that the current climate in this country is particularly oriented towards industry, as opposed to finance. Managerial jobs in industry, however responsible, command neither the pay nor glamour of jobs in the financial sector. Industry does not attract the brightest students. The fashionable ethos owes more to the competitive short-term dealing ethos of the financial world than the need to work together for the long haul which characterises successful industrial projects – however often the Chancellor may use the phrase 'long-term'.

American influences

Elliott and Atkinson analyse the influence of American political thinking on Tony Blair and other key New Labour figures. Labour and the Democrats share the problem of being parties of government at a time when government everywhere is in retreat. Clinton and Blair have taken the 1960s mixture of economic interventionism and social liberalism and turned it on its head, pushing social authoritarianism into the vacuum left by the surrender of

economic policy to the dictates of global capitalism. Blair's desire to make British party politics more like those in the US is dangerous because democracy becomes sterile and ultimately meaningless if there is no clash of ideological belief – and, I would add, clash of interests.

Constitutional reform

The authors are critical of New Labour's preoccupation with constitutional reform, as a diversion from the more urgent task of tilting the economic mechanism back in favour of working people and the poor. Labour election manifestos in the 1980s were concerned with reducing unemployment and said little about constitutional reform. In the 1990s the emphasis became reversed. They warn of the pitfalls of constitutional modernisation on the grounds that nothing dates as quickly as last year's political fashion, quoting examples from post-war European constitutions. Moreover, there appears to be a dangerous desire to rewire the constitution in such a way as to bypass the electorate, or at any rate their elected representatives.

Full employment

The authors recognise that the best way to bring the bargaining power of employees and employers into some sort of balance is to run the economy at a high level of demand. But they do not go on to discuss how this can be achieved whilst keeping inflation in check, for example by pay policies, nor the possible complications for sterling or the trade balance.

The shift in the social balance away from the ordinary worker and towards the better-off stemmed originally from the abandonment of full employment in response to the inflationary crisis in the 1970s. But the fact that Mrs Thatcher was able to win a general election with unemployment at the formerly politically inconceivable level of three million signified a changing political ethos which enabled mass unemployment to replace incomes policy as a means of moderating pay increases and keeping down inflation. I believe that the shift in power in favour of managers and the better-off that followed continued heavy unemployment also had an insidious attitude to questions of inequality and social justice. To give one example, current levels of pay for top directors would have been unthinkable in earlier years because the potential critics one way or another wielded some power in industry and the community. But by the 1990s, these objectors could be brushed aside.

Europe

The authors' analysis of the European Union is strongly hostile to the whole concept of any form of governmental activity on a European scale. It is easy to see the grounds for opposition to such initiatives as Maastricht and EMU which are based on an unacceptable economic philosophy. It is more difficult to understand their thesis that the Union as such has nothing to offer in terms of the fulfilment of the left's objectives. If we are seeking means to control our own economic destiny, then it would seem self evident that the increasingly integrated European economy needs appropriate democratic governmental machinery for determining economic policy at a European level. An independent European Central Bank does not fit this role and is a manifestation of monetarist dogma. But the Keynesian alternative needs a European federal government. The case for a common European foreign and defence policy is working towards the same end. (It is, incidentally, difficult to understand the authors' thesis that the European Union is a unitary state in embryo rather than a federation, merely because the Commission has issued so many detailed directives on matters which, it could be argued, should be settled at a national level.)

There are two distinct questions. The first is: at a time when other European governments' policies are dominated by neo-liberal economic thinking, should the UK retain the degree of independence needed to follow policies aiming to restore full employment? The answer is almost certainly yes; and the experience of the last few years shows that it is still possible for the UK to expand while continental countries are in a period of deflation. The second and longer-term question is: if other European governments were to eschew the new orthodoxy and follow more expansionary policies, would we gain by being a full member of the club? I would say yes. The authors' implied answer is no.

International organisations

Similar issues arise in regard to international institutions. The authors stigmatise the IMF, GATT and the WTO as mere instruments of big business. But surely the correct diagnosis is that such institutions are controlled by the governments of the most powerful nations and merely reflect the prevailing economic doctrines. It is not the existence of these organisations that is the problem, but the political complexion and economic philosophy of the governments concerned. After all, the Bretton Woods institutions set up at the end of World War Two were originally an integral part of an international Keynesian approach designed to ensure greater stability in the world economy and maintain full employment.

Where should we go next?

Like most revolutionary books, from Karl Marx's *Capital* to Will Hutton's *The State We're In*, this one is much stronger on demolition than construction. Their general answer to the problem of global insecurity appears to be that we should retreat into the nation state, because only at this level of government can democracy prevail and the interests of the many take ascendancy over those of big business. But if national governments were to be imbued with a philosophy no longer dominated by big business, the approach of international organisations would also change. Again there are two levels of argument. In the short-term, how can a lone social democratic country fare best, when most of the others are following neo-liberal deflationary policies? Can and should it put up the shutters and isolate itself from world deflation? This is the question which appeared to face many countries in the 1930s and led to self-defeating protection and competitive devaluation. The Bretton Woods agreement was designed to prevent this happening again, and so

answer in a positive way the second question: how can we avert these dangers collectively?

Globalisation has now overtaken the Bretton Woods settlement, and the world economy has once again become vulnerable to highly volatile movements of capital. There is, moreover, an inherent contradiction between industry organised on a global scale and violently fluctuating exchange rates which make it impossible for multi-national companies to plan their investment and operations rationally. There is in my view an urgent need for a 'New Bretton Woods' tackling the problems of speculative capital movements and exchange rate instability, hand in hand with the development of stronger prudential regulation of banks and other financial institutions on an international scale. The authors imply that we should not attempt to do this, because any such organisations are liable to be controlled by governments and officials with whose economic philosophy we disagree. But this merely accentuates the need to achieve an intellectual counter-revolution, just as the monetarists and neo-liberals captured official thinking in the 1980s.

The dominance of the free market approach and its emphasis on minimising the role of government has set back the development of world governance just when an advance was becoming overdue. There is now less impetus to build up international institutions than there was fifty years ago, even though the need is greater than ever. While the authors make the case for the prosecution most effectively, they do not in my view ask the right questions about what we should be doing when the current offenders have been put away. As I see it, the challenge we face both in the economic and political fields is how to make international organisations more effective and more democratic.

Given the number of countries and people involved, this raises fascinating and difficult problems. We have to strike a balance between the need for relatively small bodies like the G7, or even the Security Council, for effective leadership on the one hand, and safeguarding the interests of the vast array of poorer people in developing countries on the other. Some of the ingenuity deployed in building up the hybrid constitution of the EU with its unique combination of Commission, Council of Ministers and Parliament now needs to be applied to constitution building on a global scale. At the same time we need to be devising peacekeeping environmental and economic policies at global, regional, national and (where appropriate) local levels. That I would suggest is the positive response to the Age of Insecurity which this volume so effectively describes.

■Barry Quirk

Civic Entrepreneurship, Charles Leadbeater and Sue Goss (Public Management Foundation / Demos 1998).

For public institutions to be successful they must be both well governed and well managed. The Government is rightly paying a lot of attention to improving how public institutions are governed. The pace and scale of constitutional change is breath-taking. Witness the implementation of democratic renewal at the sub-national level through devolution alongside the promotion of new style Mayors and Cabinets for local government. This agenda (alongside electoral reform) is crucial to reconnect public institutions to the citizens they serve and to strengthen the chains of accountability between the public and politicians at both national and local level.

But renewing democracy is hollow if public institutions deliver inefficient, ineffective and inequitable services. Modern public institutions need excellence in both governance and in management. And this is where Leadbeater and Goss address a neglected issue for this government. For their booklet addresses the issue of 'civic entrepreneurs'; active, purposeful public sector managers who work with social purpose. And in so doing they have identified a key area for the modernising project: the modernisation of public sector management.

The nineteenth century French economist Jean Baptiste Say defined an 'entrepreneur' as someone who 'uses resources in new ways to maximise productivity and effectiveness'. This notion of reconfiguring resources in an adaptive way purposefully to take account of opportunities lies at the heart of entrepreneurship. It was used by Osborne and Gaebler in their 1992 book *Reinventing Government*, and it underpins this publication.

Leadbeater and Goss take the argument further than Osborne and Gaebler, although the approach they adopt is very similar. They show how it is not enough for public managers to act with social purpose; they need first to establish a legitimacy to act. Through a number of case studies they show how entrepreneurs make improvements regardless of the contexts and constraints in which they work. Almost half of the ninety pages is taken up with an examination of entrepreneurship, in places such as the Thames Valley Police; West Walker primary school in Newcastle upon Tyne; the Dorset Health Authority; and two local councils in England: Kirklees and South Somerset.

Like all entrepreneurs, the public sector managers have a positive 'can do' approach. But they don't just want to do anything. They are always searching for how social capital can be optimised, how social improvements are best achieved. They are not looking to maximise the return on the capital invested but to raise the social impact of the resources they are deploying. Leadbeater and Goss argue that if the Government's ambitious social goals in education, employment, crime and health are to be achieved it will be essential to harness the talents of many thousands of civic entrepreneurs to raise the public sector to new levels of effectiveness.

And they are right in pointing to the essential characteristics of entrepreneurial organisations. They don't ask 'why', they ask 'why not?' These organisations have cultures which continually pose (and answer) fundamental questions about purpose and performance. 'What are we trying to achieve? How do we intend to achieve it? Does our plan to achieve these goals seem plausible to all our partners and users? How do we manage the risks inherent in this change?'

Civic entrepreneurs are restless, creative, lateral thinking rule breakers. Sometimes their organisations have given them political permission and managerial authority to act; in other cases, the entrepreneurs create the space to act and ask for 'forgiveness' afterwards. As operators, they blend visionary thinking with an appetite for opportunism. Somewhat troubling for the Government (with its ever growing and understandable requirement for plans) they usually work by having strategic goals and not strategic plans. Ask an entrepreneur to show you his or her plan and they will probably say they don't have one.

Leadbeater and Goss show, however, that the actions of entrepreneurs are not simply managerial, but political. And this is where they depart from the earlier work of Osborne and Gaebler and add a further dimension. For them, civic entrepreneurs are only successful if they win consent for change. They need to build a licence to innovate. After all they are innovating with public money and therefore they require public legitimacy to act and they must show how their actions improve the public accountability of the institutions in which they operate.

In this way civic entrepreneurship is about political renewal as much as it is about managerial change. Public institutions both deliver services and manage public risks. To improve their productivity and accountability at the same time is difficult; but this is the 'win-win' that government is looking to achieve.

Leadbeater and Goss are correct to

focus on the quality of public sector management. To be successful, public managers need first, to win a mandate for innovation and risk taking and second, they need to reconfigure resources to deliver higher social value and more social capital. This requires skills of the highest order. These issues demand proper attention from government. If we are to have a University for Industry, why not a University for Governance? Sustainable competitiveness and improved productivity are issues for the civic as well as the private entrepreneur. But the dimensions of equity and public accountability require additional skills of the civic entrepreneurs of the future. Leadbeater and Goss's analysis is correct and their prescription – of learning from the best; improving the quality of management; and focusing on outcomes – is also sensible.

But perhaps something more can be learned from a continuing American debate on 'refounding public administration'. In the early 1980s there was a recognition amongst some American public theorists that public institutions had lost their way. Single purpose public institutions were focusing on service performance to the exclusion of public accountability. Moreover, public sector experts (in planning, health, resource allocation and the like) were exercising increasing power and authority outside of debates in the public realm about how risks should be managed and what was in the public interest.

This American debate is not simply about how to promote entrepreneurship (*pace* Osborne and Gaebler) into the public sector. Rather, it argues that public managers have a key role in facilitating and educating the public to decide things for themselves. Civic entrepreneurs win a licence to innovate to deliver better public services with the public's money. Civic educators help citizens to decide for themselves how to balance risks and how to come to judgement about what is the public interest. If the arguments of the American 'refounding' movement have merit, public managers will need to be policy advisors, civic entrepreneurs as well as being public educators. In that case, perhaps the University for Governance is not such a wacky idea.

Leadbeater and Goss have fulfilled a major task: they have shown that the public sector has plenty of entrepreneurs: people throughout the country putting resources to optimum use for social purpose in the communities they serve. And in so doing, the authors have shown that the public sector is far more innovative than most people imagine.

Osborne and Gaebler (1992), *Reinventing Government*
Walmsley, G and Wolf J (eds) (1996), *Refounding Democratic Public Administration*

Become a subscriber ...

Renewal is a journal of politics, movements and ideas. A quarterly journal committed to political modernisation, it has been the bible of researchers, parliamentary candidates, party officials and academic advisers on new Labour's inside track.

Why not subscribe?
1999 subscription rates are (for four issues):

Individual subscriptions
UK £25 – Rest of the World £30

Institutional subscriptions
UK £50 – Rest of the World £55

Please send me one year's subscription, starting with Issue No. _____

I enclose payment of £ _____

Name _____

Address _____

_____

_____ Postcode _____

Please return this form (a copy will do) with a cheque or money order made payable to *Renewal*. Send to: *Renewal*, c/o Lawrence & Wishart, 99a Wallis Road, London E9 5LN.

Back issues

Out of print

Vol 1 No 1, Vol 2 No 1, Vol 2 No 2, Vol 3 No 2, Vol 3 No 3, Vol 4 No 1 & Vol 4 No 2

Back issues cost £6.00 each (including postage) and are available from:
Lawrence & Wishart
99a Wallis Road, London E9 5LN